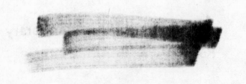

A Quest for Discipleship
Father Claude Buchanan

Servants of the Paraclete

magnificat press
Avon-by-the-Sea, NJ

A Quest for Discipleship was published in longer form in the *Newsletter* of the Servants of the Paraclete from 1979 through 1986. It was published by them in binder format under the title *Primacy of Service: A Quest for Discipleship.*

Printed in the United States of America
ISBN 0-940543-03-6
Library of Congress catalog card number: 87-070016
Magnificat Press
Avon, NJ 07717

Contents

Preface

A *Quest for Discipleship* was first published in the newsletter of the Servants of the Paraclete. When the first newsletter was written almost eleven years ago it was just that—a newsletter. The first edition totaled fifty copies. We really didn't know what to do with so many. Now it is mailed each month to nearly 25,000 people. I hope that it provides practical suggestions for living out the mission and message of Jesus.

I would like to thank a number of people for their continued support, but rather than miss anyone I will simply say, "Thanks." This thanks extends most importantly to you, the readers, who over the years have become cherished friends. I pray that God will bless each and every one of you abundantly in all things, small and great, bright and beautiful.

Father Claude Buchanan
Servants of the Paraclete
Il Ritiro (the Little Retreat)
Dittmer, Missouri

The Magnificat

(Luke 1:46-55)

My soul proclaims the greatness of the Lord, my spirit rejoices in God my Savior; for He has looked with favor on His lowly servant.

From this day all generations will call me blessed: the Almighty has done great things for me, and holy is His name.

He has mercy on those who fear Him in every generation.

He has shown the strength of His arm, He has scattered the proud in their conceit.

He has cast down the mighty from their thrones, and has lifted up the lowly.

He has filled the hungry with good things, and the rich He has sent away empty.

He has come to the help of His servant Israel, for He has remembered His promise of mercy, the promise He had made to our fathers, to Abraham and his children forever.

1

The Primacy of Service

When the alarm goes off early in the morning I find it a real struggle to pull myself from the warmth of the covers. After more than twenty-five years in the priesthood I hit the deck uncertain of the new day and the demands it will surely present. I think of the priest who called a few nights ago. His first words were, "I'm just tired of giving." As the new day dawns his words come to mind. The successes and failures of yesterday are past history. Today is mine to strive again to "put on the mind of Christ." The day may get off to a slow start but I am ever thankful for the opportunities it will afford to think as He would think, to speak as He would speak, to act as He would act.

I join my community for morning prayer. I beg for an increase in faith. Little of what I will do this day will bear visible results. I can no longer lean too heavily on the natural satisfactions so present in the early days of my priesthood. My faith must grow in abundance so I can see, hear and feel God's presence in myself, in my surroundings and in those I am called to serve.

After morning prayer one of our guest fathers asked for a few moments of my time—just to talk. As a servant of the Paraclete I have heard the story so many times, but for the priest who now sits before me what he has to say is all-important, unique. He is precious in the Lord. I listen as I would wish to be listened to in my time of need.

Later I make a trip to the airport to meet a priest confused in the mind and heart. As he walks down the concourse I try my best to see through his untidy appearance, the defeated look. In faith I know his hands have ministered life unto many. In the silence of my heart I beg God that he again will experience the joy, the fullness of loving service.

It is my turn to prepare the evening meal. I'm convinced this is a holy task. Over the entrance of our dining room we formerly had a small sign that read, "Good food is good for the soul." When the dining room was redecorated the sign disappeared. I miss it. A man can come to the table burdened with the weight of many problems, enjoy a well-prepared meal and go away refreshed in mind and heart.

The father who arrived this day is silent at the evening meal. It is impossible at this time to break through his hurt, his confusion. Just being present to him is all I can offer at the moment.

There are those precious moments throughout the day and especially in the evening hours when I can truly lift my mind and heart to my Father. Time to get my head on straight and hope for a better tomorrow. I may find some way to build a bridge of understanding and trust with the priest that arrived this day. He feels very much alone tonight. Possibly tomorrow he will find a brother.

It is a struggle to live out our calling no matter what the particular ministry might be. I personally find that the joys of my priesthood far outweigh the sorrows. My life is nothing too great but it is in these everyday happenings that I am called to work out my salvation. I can honestly stand before my community this day—you stand before your people—and say loud and clear with Paul, "I live now, not I, but Christ lives in me"; at least I'm trying—you are too.

I need to reflect more on my motives for answering the call of my Master. Truly I have been chosen to be another Christ in my day. In no uncertain terms I am here this day to seek to be of service to all and in no way to seek first to be served. As day follows night, in giving of my time, my energy, my very self in loving service, I too will receive.

I may need to laugh more at my own failures so I can honestly accept myself with all my limitations. It is a wise and holy man who knows both his strengths and his weaknesses. The greatness of my own spirit will be revealed in my willingness to make those changes in my personal life that will enable me to be a clearer channel of grace to my people. Then the power of my Master will flow abundantly in me. My energy, endurance, courage and capacity to love will rise and take hold of every fiber of my being.

All this will help me to look beyond my own little world so I might daily enrich the lives of others. To be big in mind and heart is a precious blessing, one to be ever grateful for. It is easy to become, often unknowingly, a victim of my own little fantasies, my own particular view of life.

To become more sharing, giving, loving, I need to feel more the joys and sorrow, the successes and failures, the ambitions and goals of my people. I need to go beyond measure in my concern for my people if I am to find enduring fulfillment in my calling. Each one of us has someone—family or friends—entrusted to our love, to our service. In a spirit of giving I will make greater effort to be attentive to their problems. What may at times seem very insignificant to me, possibly a tale of woe I have heard many times over, will take on real importance if I am sensitive to the hurt of the person seeking my help. My body language will also reveal my true concern. There will be no hurried movements, no quick glances at my watch, no impressions given that I have more important things to do. I desire in the Spirit of my Master that the person before me leave my presence more at peace for our common experience, ready to face the harshness of life's problems with a deeper faith and far greater courage.

If I fail to live out my calling in this spirit of loving concern, there is a real risk that I will become disenchanted with what my vocation is all about. I will then begin to seek my fulfillment in "perishable things," the fringe benefits of my calling. I may remain in the priesthood but find myself void of spirit and life. I will then have failed to taste the sweetness of the Lord. I could very well end my days a crotchety old bachelor zeroed in on myself. When calling to mind the initial sacrifices made in accepting His call I think how tragic it would be to end my days frustrated and resentful. The young who aspire to the call of the priesthood would be turned off by the example of my life.

In my quest to live out my priestly calling more abundantly I find myself in constant need of new beginnings. It is my firm resolve to make greater effort to seek first the kingdom of God in myself so my words, my actions will reveal a far greater appreciation of my commitment and a more intense faith life.

To honestly put first things first in my life, I intend to set meaningful goals that are truly Christ-centered goals each day—even if I find it necessary to write them down at the beginning of the day.

Then I will take practical steps to implement my resolves this very day. Like the recovering alcoholic, I will live one day at a time. Half-baked plans, confused goals and unaccomplished good intentions are the result of poor planning. Without a consistent conscious effort to use the precious time that is mine, my daily life can become most frustrating and my priestly existence mediocre at best.

With this new beginning at hand it is good for me to reflect on what it means to be a servant in the likeness of Jesus. I can choose to serve in two ways. I can serve at my convenience, which keeps me in the driver's seat. In this manner of serving I choose when, where, and whom I will serve. This is not the primacy of service demanded by Jesus. It is for me to be available when, where and to whom the Spirit directs. Without any doubt this notion of service will leave me most vulnerable, but only then will I personally experience true freedom and taste the sweetness of the Lord. I will lose the fear of being used, manipulated or taken advantage of. With Paul I will spend myself and be spent for the kingdom of God, no matter what the personal cost.

I ask for the creative power to use my God-given imagination to discern my Christian commitment for this day. It may be letters to be written. I can never underestimate the religious value of a letter that reveals to the receiver that someone does care.

This day I will visit a young lady dying of cancer. For her I represent the link between the earth she knows, the warm touch of love, the familiar sounds heard, the good times experienced and the heaven she believes in. My frequent visits will help her to accept what she cannot change and strengthen her faith in things to come.

I beg for a greater spirit of compassion to feel in some way the pain, the disappointment, the helplessness, the boredom, the doubt and unbelief that is the real condition of so many who seek my guidance. Let me ever be a willing listener. Then may I inspire them by my words from an outpouring of sensitivity grounded in a vibrant faith life.

When someone asks for remembrance in my prayers, may I look upon this request as sacred. When asked in prayer to remember a special need, I am called upon to be a mediator between the visible world of feeling, seeing and touching and the God who for now remains invisible.

My most difficult endeavor is to see all men created to the image and likeness of God. I will give special consideration to those who in some way turn me off, those I may find totally indifferent to my efforts in their behalf. I must seek out those weak in faith, look for imaginative ways to bring the Good News to those who have not had the opportunity to know their God.

In all my endeavors I will find those precious moments to lift my mind and heart to my Lord in an honest, straightforward manner, ever conscious that I am to work through Him, with Him and in Him.

As I grow older, I become more aware of a primacy that is at the very core of Christian belief: *primacy of service.* The primacy of service so exemplified in the life of Jesus can easily be overlooked or taken for granted when I become busy about many things of far less importance.

"By this will all men know you are my disciples: That you love one another as I have loved you." I know full well the extent of Jesus' love. "No greater love has a man than he give his life for his friend." This Jesus did for you, for me. He urges me to love all as He has loved me. I think of the mother standing at the bedside of her dying daughter. She would willingly give her own life so her daughter might live. I know a father who works three jobs so he can provide for his family of ten children. I call to mind the young soldier in Vietnam who threw himself over his wounded buddy to shield him from further hurt. I know a priest who, for many years, in a leper colony, gave of himself with few tangible signs of success or even recognition. "No greater love has a man than he give his life for his friend." Faith in the love revealed by Jesus on the cross urges me on to greater things in the spirit.

Lord, grant me sensitivity of mind and heart to be ever conscious of the joys and the sorrows, the successes and the defeats, the ambitions and the unattained goals of all those who enter my life this day. Grant me the strength of purpose to so enrich their lives by a living, vibrant faith in the mission of Jesus. Then we will begin to experience here and now a foretaste of the kingdom.

St. Francis de Sales said, "How blessed it is to love in this life as we will someday love in the next." Many friends and benefactors have been inspired to share their own joys and sorrows with me, and my faith is constantly strengthened when I witness the miracles of grace worked in the lives of ordinary people who have taken to heart the words of Jesus to love others as they so want to be loved themselves.

The mission and message of Jesus are revealed in the midst of the everyday happenings of family living—preparing the children for school, shopping, concern if there will be enough left over for the mortgage bill, fuel bill and unforeseen emergencies, caring for an elderly parent, forcing yourself to make one more sales call with the hope of easing the burden of the week's expenses, finding time to work Saturday's bingo, waiting to hear the familiar footsteps of a teenager returning home from a late date on the weekend, being ever sensitive to all those little things that help strengthen a loving relationship between husband and wife.

Sometimes I seriously wonder at the complexity of my daily life. There are the calls to be made, the deadlines to be met, the financial problems to be solved, the salaries to be paid, the taxes to be withheld, the time given to necessary repairs on the plant. I wonder if all these concerns prevent me from living out more fully the mission and the message of Jesus.

When I am able to steal some moments for silent prayer, I simply ask for the wisdom to see clearly those gifts of the human spirit so necessary to living out the Christian life. These gifts are easily overlooked yet so vital if we are to reveal Jesus, His Spirit, to our brothers and sisters.

I ask for the gift of listening, a presence that radiates through my concern for the individual now before me. He is the most important person in my life at this moment. I will not rush him. I will not plan my response. I will just listen.

Strangely enough, I pray for the gift of letting people alone. Every person needs times of quiet. I will respect the gift of solitude, of privacy for those who desire to be alone with their God.

I ask for the gift of prayer for myself and for my brothers and sisters. I will lift up my mind and heart in prayer for all, but especially for those who ask for my help in prayer. By doing this I am saying, "You are important to me."

Letter writing is an important facet of my priestly ministry. Much good goes undone by the person who simply says, "I am not a letter writer." An encouraging letter can change the day for someone suffering in mind and heart, can bring great joy to an otherwise burdened heart. Letter writing for me often provides the means of revealing the Good News to many in a profound and lasting way. The written word endures. I pray for the gift of correspondence.

I pray for a cheerful spirit. Psychologists say our moods change thirty times a day. I must be careful not to inflict my changing moods on others. I should not fill my day with complaints, harsh judgments, pessimistic predictions. In the midst of the most chaotic conditions, I need to search for what is good. A cheerful smile, words of encouragement or just making the best of a bad situation will be my goal.

I will look for those opportunities to compliment my people for tasks well done. So many serve faithfully for many years with little, if any, recognition. I will be quick to identify personal strengths in my brothers and sisters and urge them on to greater things in the spirit.

I will seek out those occasions wherein I can anticipate a thoughtful gesture. I will not wait till I stumble upon good deeds to be done. I will anticipate acts of charity I can readily perform this day. I will not leave menial tasks to others. I can wash dishes, help clean the hall, prepare a meal for an unexpected guest. I will continually keep before my mind that I am called to be a servant in the full Christian sense of the word. Whatever I do for my brothers and sisters I do unto Him.

These I am sure are but a few human gifts we so desperately need in order to make the Spirit of Jesus live here and now. I ask God that these gifts may be yours in abundance. On my part, I beg to know the moments when I can be present to my neighbor as Jesus is present to me.

Not long ago I was speaking with an elderly priest friend of mine whom I respect highly not only as a good friend but as a priest. He had just made his annual retreat. He expressed to me his dissatisfaction with all the emphasis the retreat master placed on love. "He should have hit us between the eyes with more hell and brimstone—get us back on track."

I could readily appreciate where my priest friend was coming from. In the past, fear of a stern, angry God was often used to move the faithful to observe the commandments, the admonitions of Jesus, the laws of the Church. Without any doubt this approach was successful to some degree. However, when fear is used to urge people to action we often end up like the Sadducees and the Pharisees with the letter of the law being observed with spirit and life missing. When we fail to act out of love we run the great risk of doing what appears to be good for the wrong reasons. "The last temptation is the greatest treason: To do the right deed for the wrong reason"—T. S. Elliot. We also fail to bring the best out in our people. The tremendous potential to love that rests in the heart of every person can easily be thwarted by fear. Someone wisely said, "The worst way to improve the world is to condemn it." For all the wrong we see around us today there are also the countless daily miracles of ordinary people whose sacrifice and giving spirits reveal the love of Jesus.

God is love. It was God who so loved the world that He sent His Son into our midst that we may not perish but have life more abundantly.

For some reason my priest friend's remark rested uneasy with me. We speak today much about love but so often fail to grasp the full significance of what it really means to love as Jesus loved. To love in the truest and richest sense, as Jesus would have us love, is no easy task. "By this will all men know you are my disciples, that you love one another as I have loved you." These words of the Master should be branded into the heart of every Christian who desires to walk in His footsteps. "As I have loved you."

In the Spirit of Jesus I am called as a Christian, even more so as a priest, to be a servant. My spirit of giving, of loving, can in no way be limited to those who readily appreciate my service, to those who willingly love me in return. My love cannot be restricted to the ones who are always ready and willing to share with me in our common Christian commitment.

The love Jesus places before me demands an open heart to the unloveable, the lonely person who has never experienced what it means to be loved, the person who rarely thinks of God, the person who actually spurns God's love and my attempt to love. It is not easy to love the person who is constantly stirring the pot of discontent, to love the know-it-all, to love the person who is zeroed in on himself to the total forgetfulness of others, to love the person who is using me for his own ends, to love someone in authority who is manipulating those under him for his own satisfaction. This is especiallly true when the person we are dealing with is using the "will of God" to back up his own selfish goals. The temptations of religion are many.

When we read the words of Jesus we cannot help but be impressed with Jesus' belief in people and His willingness to travel the long road with them. I cannot help but think of Peter, who denied His Master three times the night before His crucifixion. Peter had walked with Jesus for three years. He had witnessed His miracles, Jesus healing the sick, giving sight to the blind, having the cripple walk again, but—above all—seeing with his own eyes Jesus lift the burden of sin and despair from the shoulders of so many. Yet, when the cards were down, Peter walked away denying he even knew the Man. Peter was readily forgiven. He went on to give his own life for his belief in Jesus.

I am severely tempted at times just to give up on an individual who seems to be going no place. I find myself desiring to move on to someone who will present fewer demands on my time and energy. It is for me on these occasions to reflect on the spiritual truth that all men and women are created to the image and likeness of God, examples of the Spirit no matter how poorly they reveal this truth. Only faith in Jesus, His words, His example can keep me ever conscious of this all-embracing reality.

The needs of some of my people will demand getting together over an extended period of time. In the brief encounters, in the extended meetings, I am asked to help other pilgrims work out their relationship with the world they live in, the people they meet, the God we adore. I am asked to assist others in faith to overcome, to triumph. Without any doubt this is one of the most sacred missions of my calling — to help others live at peace with themselves, with their brothers and sisters, with their God.

There are three fundamental truths I keep in mind; if I fail to observe these truths, those I serve can become just routine business and my approach will fast become condescending. With all the experience garnered over the years it is easy to consider myself all-knowing. How can I avoid this?

First of all, I stand in wonder before the person in my presence. Every meeting with another—even a brief encounter—is a privilege. As a shepherd I have the opportunity to see hidden glory, the suppressed potential to love, grace untouched.

I am prepared to marvel! The person before me, revealing nobility and goodness, however burdened with worry, is made in the image of God. This nervous, slouching body before me is a temple of the Spirit. Jesus would have suffered His entire passion and death for just this person. This is an awesome truth. I am prepared, in faith, to admire, to respect, to revere the person now in my presence.

Second, I must be prepared to admit that I know little of the workings of the spirit of the person now before me. There are years of many and varied experiences I have no knowledge of. There are feelings of past joy and anger, of faith and despair, that will never be shared with me. There are dreams of accomplishments that so often in reality fall short of our expectations. I may be tempted at times to spill out answers—stock answers that fail to meet the needs of the unique individual before me. I too must listen to the Spirit. Little by little, bit by bit, the vision of Jesus will be revealed in the person before me. I will walk at the side of my brother or sister, encouraging him or her to accept the vision of Jesus. I will help remove the obstacles preventing real growth in the spirit of Christian commitment. Radical changes may be demanded by the prompting of the Spirit. I will be there to encourage, to urge on when the path becomes rough. We will be as two pilgrims walking together.

I am more and more convinced that when someone comes to me for assistance in living out more fully the Christian commitment, he is seeking a greater union with God in prayer. If anyone truly seeks to know the Master—to know His will—it will be revealed in prayer, in conversation with God. With a sincere heart, God's vision for him will become real. The obstacles preventing the vision's fulfillment will be made manifest and the strength to bring about those necessary changes from within will be given. The beginnings of a new person will emerge. Knock and it shall be opened; seek and you shall find; that is an infallible promise made by Jesus.

If I am to walk in the presence of the Lord with another person, then I am called basically to help my brother or sister to grow in appreciation of the tremendous power of prayer, to urge them to seek the company of the living God, to live in His presence. When a person reveals himself in honest prayer, only then will great things be worked in him. It is easy to speak of self-giving tasks, formulas of prayer, new approaches in the quest for the Spirit, but, when all is said and done, it is through maturity in prayer—total reliance on God in faith—that we come face to face with our God. Only then will we become ever sensitive to the working of the Spirit so that every task, small and great, will not only have meaning now but also transcendent value.

I assist others ever conscious that my conversation takes place in God's active presence. Walking hand in hand with my brothers and sisters, I desire to live all the days of my life in His company.

I am called to be a servant willing to give freely of my time, my energy, my very being in loving service. I have been called to serve and not seek to be served. My desire to be a servant in imitation of my Master demands a clear understanding of my calling. It demands a compassionate heart that will graciously embrace all, the mighty and powerful, the poor and rejected, the committed Christian and the indifferent, those who appeal to me and those who turn me off. "God wills the salvation of all men and women." When this truth of Jesus' message becomes a reality in my life as a man called to spiritual leadership, then, and then alone, will I walk in the footsteps of my Master in the fullness of my calling as "another Christ."

2

The Time Is Now

I often find myself dreaming of the ideal time to put my hands to the plow and to become the saint I am called to be. When this particular project is completed; when I lose thirty pounds and have a more asthetic look; when my term as Treasurer General is completed; when the day comes for me to pass on the responsibilities of my office to another and I am presented with my retirement watch; when I no longer feel married to the telephone; when I find time to spend in our hermitage; when all these nice things happen then I will have the opportunity to get myself together and live for Jesus and Jesus alone. Hope springs eternal in all human beings that when conditions are near perfect the opportunity to achieve what we really want to do will be present. Unfortunately, I find myself thinking of this ideal situation and fail to face the realilty — the profound truth — that holiness of life for me will only be attained in the here-and-now of my daily existence. There are moments to lift my mind and heart to my God in prayer even in the midst of many necessary distractions. Solitude is not so much a matter of place but an attitude of mind. I am called to do what I can, where I am, with what I have to give.

This calls to mind the story of an African farmer who sold his farm and spent the rest of his life hunting diamonds the world over, only to have the richest diamond mine in the world discovered on the farm he sold.

When I find myself dreaming about greener pastures I ask for the wisdom to see the untold opportunities hidden in my daily life from the moment my feet hit the floor in the early morning till the gift of sleep comes at night. If I receive the gift to lift up someone in the spirit, to be more loving, more giving, then I know God has accomplished great things in me. When I consider how precious each person is that crosses my path every waking hour, it would take forever and a day to love them tenderly, to walk at their sides as a fellow pilgrim. In this spirit the smallest happening becomes significant, truly a moment of grace.

An elderly priest once told me that the most woeful two words he had heard were "if only". *If only* I had done things differently — or not done them at all. *If only* I had not lost my temper and said such cruel words. *If only* I had not made such a dishonest move. *If only* I had not been so selfish. *If only* I had not told that hurtful lie. *"If only...."*

During my early days in the seminary, I would spend the summer months working at our family-owned mortuary. When a family would come to view the deceased for the first time, we would always make it a point to be at their side to comfort them in their immediate grief. So often I would hear the words, "If only Mom could see these beautiful flowers." "If only I had visited with my dad more often." "If only..." It would be easy to list a litany of *if only* expressions. If the deceased person could speak again but for a few moments, I am sure there would be regrets for the many precious moments wasted when so much good could have been accomplished—words of encouragement expressed to a son who had met temporary defeat; words of praise and appreciation for a wife or husband for tasks well done but so often taken for granted; a sharing of temporal possessions with those in dire need. There is always a tendency to hold onto material possessions, fearing a future loss of security.

The trouble with *if only* is that it does not change anything. It keeps a person headed in the wrong direction — backward instead of forward. It wastes precious time. In the end, if a person lets it become a way of life, it fast becomes a real roadblock to any spiritual growth.

The greatest substitute for the *if only* attitude is a *next time* attitude — my willingness to change.

"Without Him I can do nothing," but in my humble prayer God can do great things in me. I take heart. There will be, God willing, a *next time.*

When my final hours approach and my time of service comes to an end, I pray there will be no serious regrets. In these precious hours I wish only to have abundant trust that He will be merciful to me, knowing that I have made every effort to love much even though I have stumbled along the way many times. He has been ever at my side to help me struggle with the next time. Lord, grant me the insight to see myself for what I am and the inner courage to become what I ought to be.

A minister friend of mine patterned his entire life with his family and his flock around a Scripture quote, "This is the appointed time" (Ps. 102:14). My minister friend looks for every opportunity with graciousness of heart to sing of the kingdom and let those entrusted to his care know of the unexpected beauty of the Christian challenge, a beauty that uplifts, gives hope and inspires the hearts of those it touches.

To accomplish this in my life, I too must be ever conscious that the moment before me *is* the appointed time.

This is the appointed time to give generously to others of what I really have no need of. A few days ago I was standing at the service counter of a discount store. A young man and woman were putting some school clothes on layaway. The entire amount was just a little over twenty dollars. I asked the clerk if I could pay for the pants and shirts and let the family take the few items home without worrying about another payment before the items could be theirs to use for the school year. It was the appointed time to share. As St. Augustine said, "If you have surplus clothes, food, or money, it belongs to the less fortunate."

This is the appointed time to send your heartfelt thanks to someone who has been most thoughtful, the time to write a few lines to someone hurting in body and soul and who desperately needs to know that someone cares and is giving time in prayer for their recovery. The power of the written word can be a mighty force with enduring significance. It has the power to bring joy, forgiveness, encouragement, and hope into an otherwise depressing experience. Not much has to be said — just a genuine expression of concern. At the end of each day I make it a point to send out a few handwritten notes to those to whom I owe a word of thanks; to someone having a rough time through sickness, loneliness, defeat; or just an expression of enduring friendship. In the back of my mind I have the thought, "Although we are miles apart we are ever close in prayer."

This is the appointed time to visit one who has suffered the loss of husband or wife, brother or sister, son or daughter a few weeks ago. Once the crowds have gone, the immediate support so evident at the death of a loved one often fades. The world must go on. People are forced to return to the tasks of everyday living. What a consolation to one filled with grief to receive the gift of an unexpected visit from one who is sensitive to all that it means to lose a daughter or son, a husband or wife who had been present at your side so many years. Most of us never fully realize the deep love, the preciousness of friendship, devotion and loyalty of a loved one until we no longer have them.

This is the appointed time to seek out those who need words of encouragement, someone to listen to them or to just stand at their side. I'm thinking of a young man, age eighteen, who just received the news that he would die of cancer within six months. He kept a stiff upper lip in front of his parents, brothers and sisters, knowing their own grief. When I came into the room — with the door closed and all the others gone — he grabbed my arm and cried for two hours. I am nothing great, but I held his hands to mine without speaking and felt his utter anguish. It was a humbling experience.

This is the appointed time to appreciate the simple things of life —a cool drink in the heat of summer; a bright sunny day when God's creation reveals itself in all its glory; the evening meal when the family gathers together not only to satisfy their hunger but to exchange the happenings of the day; times of silent prayer when the opportunity is given me to pull things together and to ask with honesty of purpose whether or not I have truly put first things first in my life this day. The thought occurred to me the other day, when I was drinking a cool glass of water, how precious is a sliver of ice placed on the tongue of someone unable to drink. I have witnessed it graphically in my own father a few days before he passed into eternity. It is a wholesome experience to reflect upon what we often take for granted both in our relationships to others and those God-given gifts without which life would be unbearable.

To realize that this is the appointed time is a tremendous blessing. It demands we live in the presence of the Lord and seize this moment to live out the mission of Jesus. In silent prayer — in times apart — we will be enlightened to what is to be accomplished in this, the appointed time.

In all honesty — acutely conscious of the contradictions I find within myself — I desire to be a saint. Jesus promised holiness to those who hunger and thirst for righteousness. Or, in the words of Thomas Merton, "We must be famished for truth." I desire above all to be receptive to God's will in my life no matter what the personal cost —triumph or defeat, ecstasy or agony.

I feel there are three basic conditions I must constantly be aware of if I am to be freed up from the rough edges of my human condition and dare to become truly a man of God. I want to genuinely know God's will.

Can I bear to face the truth about myself without deception? I ask forgiveness for so much time wasted in idle pursuits of the past, for those times I sought to serve myself at the cost of commitment to those I have been called by God to serve. I now again desire a transformation, acknowledging my utter dependence on God and the tremendous God-given potential that lies dormant within me. I am thoroughly convinced that God can do great things in me. His love can be illuminated as if through crystal, in my thoughts, my words, my actions.

This first step requires a deep sense of humility. This humility does not demand a pulling down of myself, to wallow in past failures. I am called to stand at full height so I can see something much greater than I am. The contradictions I wrestle with in myself are most evident to me not because they reveal my imperfections but because they give me a clear view of the unrealized potential for good that resides in my person — a person created in His image.

The second condition I must be aware of in my personal quest for holiness is my willingness to strive daily in prayer and in action to put aside all conflicting interest, seeking first the kingdom of God for myself and for those I am called to serve in His name. "No one can serve two masters." What are the real priorities in my life? Do I speak glibly of eternal truths but in fact seek my own deep-rooted interests?

Am I willing to reject all rival claims by false gods — the sweet taste of success, material comforts, social status? Charles de Foucauld struggled to found a religious community. He died at the hands of a thief without a single member having joined his community. However, his example brought forth the Little Brothers and Sisters of Jesus.

Single-mindedness demands a willingness on my part to remove those obstacles I know hamper me in my desire to put on the mind and heart of Jesus. If I am today what I was ten years ago, then I have failed to tackle habits so calcified within me that it would take a heavenly earthquake to move me on to greater things in the Spirit. I pray to be ever open to new insights — to an openness of the spirit permitting a full commitment to my God-given purpose to ever grow in knowledge and wisdom before God and man.

I can work so hard at developing other aspects of my life — educational achievements, social status, vocational skills — and still be content to live at a kindergarten level in the very core of my life, in everything purposeful, enduring. It is for me, for you, to strive daily to break out of our self-built tombs so we can experience a genuine tranformation in Jesus. Truly, this is the appointed time for you and I to dare to become saints.

The biggest mountain to be conquered in my quest for holiness is my need to constantly remotivate myself to seek first the kingdom of my Father. From the moment I leave the chapel in the early morning, mountains of self-concern begin to get in my way. When I fail to keep my objectives clear and my goal ' certain, contentment with old patterns of thinking and acting quickly settles in. The desire to bring about necessary change in my life weakens. It is so easy to be satisfied with the superficial acceptance of Jesus and His message—not enough to explode my soul in charity beyond measure but enough to keep me in the company of the saved. I want to take comfort in the warmth of religious experience but would at times rather avoid the everyday challenge of living out the mission and message of Jesus.

When reflecting on my one all-embracing resolution to use my allotted time more fruitfully in the service of my Lord and those entrusted to my care, I have come to realize what is necessary to remain true to my resolve. I must constantly seek a more intimate union with Jesus in prayer. The reading of Holy Scripture and other inspiring books keeps me ever conscious of my Christian commitment. I have made every effort to share my aspirations with those walking the same path in their quest for holiness, knowing that a brother helped by a brother is like a strong city.

To seek a closer union with Jesus in prayer need not for a moment be complicated. When I speak with a trusted friend, my words flow most freely. There is certainly no need to impress my friend—he knows me so well. The give-and-take of our conversations over many years has revealed my innermost thoughts. He is ever conscious of my nagging doubts, reoccurring fears, the times I have been like putty in my Master's hands, times when I have stubbornly held back, times of gratitude, times of feeling sorry for myself, times of sin, times of virtue. Through all, my friend walks at my side desiring only the best for me. In this same way I speak openly to my Lord throughout the day. Jesus said, "You are my friends."

Holy Scripture has become my constant companion. Through the daily reading of Holy Scripture the mission and the message of Jesus become more real to me with every passing day. I come in contact with His first followers, who accepted Him as the Son of God. The peer pressure to deny Him, to walk away, to remain with the saftey of the herd in condemning Him must have seemed almost overwhelming. However, they were set afire by the power of the Spirit. Nothing stood in their way. Once fearful, they were now courageous in bringing the Good News to their brothers and sisters. The witnessing power of their lives inspires me now to embrace the challenge of discipleship. I pray to follow in their footsteps, to be a servant, to think of others. I must look for a towel and pail of water.

If I am to remain true in my resolve to use the precious time given me in loving service then I am to seek out those who are intent on walking the same path. I need their encouragement when the waters become rough, when my inner convictions confront what I can feel, see and touch at this very moment. In their presence I humbly admit the sublime and the ridiculous within myself. I draw from their companionship, their listening, their insightful words, the enthusiasm to begin each new day knowing I am affirmed in His love, held in His arms and fashioned to His likeness. I have never come away from speaking with someone who is in love with Jesus — strong in faith —without being lifted up in the spirit. "Each of us will be a blessing to the other."

Lord, grant me the grace through prayer, spiritual reading and the example of my brothers and sisters to seek always to walk in your footsteps.

What I consistently put off for another time because I am busy about many things, I either value lightly or am trying to avoid. I may try to rationalize my avoidance by looking at myself as a prisoner of the many demands placed upon me. The truth of the matter is I can easily fall in love with the chains that bind me down.

On Ash Wednesday I will have the privilege of placing ashes on the foreheads of the faithful, once again calling to mind our common humanness, our common mortality. Ash Wednesday has always been one of the most meaningful days of the liturgical year for me. It reminds me personally of the rapid speed with which my time is passing. It seems but yesterday when my ordination chalice, a gift from my folks, arrived at the seminary. I raised it above my head knowing that the day long awaited was close at hand. Now I have more than twenty-five years behind me. No record for sure, but it does bring home the fact that my life-giving days as a priest are probably more than half over. I truly know neither the day nor the hour. I find myself at this time grateful for the days that have been mine.

The ashes on my forehead will bring to mind another very powerful message for me, a priest: *I now live.* This is my allotted time to share, to give, to love. I fervently pray each day for grace, the insight to live my priestly life more abundantly in loving service of those I am called to minister to in His name. As I grow older I make this urgent plea with greater determination. It is so easy to get mired in a rut of my own making. Hardening of the categories, a bachelor mentality, can easily creep into my life as a priest. I must face head-on the reality that the continued daily effort required on my part to become a more sharing, a more giving, a more loving priest will come at the cost of discipleship. In this way only can I become a more fit instrument in His service and find my own greatest fulfillment as a priest.

This is for me the precious time to seek greater understanding with those I serve, to have a more keen sensitivity to their needs in body and soul, to be more aware of where my people are coming from, to be quick to forgive, ever conscious of circumstances that can so easily change the whole picture, to be more thoughtful of the goals and ambitions of those I serve, to be more willing to go beyond convenience in the giving of my time, my energy, my very self. In this way alone will I begin again and again with each new day to taste the sweetness of the Lord.

I will not be content to be a spiritual operator. I, like you, am called to holiness. With years of service behind me, the future of my priesthood can be even more promising. You and I have, I hope, grown in wisdom and knowledge. When the day comes for my Lord to dismiss His servant, I want to part, not regretting the past, but looking forward to seeing Him face to face.

On the day of my judgement, the measure of my Christian commitment will be found in these words of Jesus: "By this will all men know you are my disciples: that you love one another as I have loved you." Have I truly made a daily effort to love as Jesus loves?

It is not in observing religious practices that I prove my love for God and for my neighbor. These religious endeavors must be *lived* to have meaning, to give real purpose to my desire to walk in the footsteps of Jesus.

Now is the most important moment because another encounter in time may not be mine. The person now before me is the most important person because I may never meet another. Serving now the needs of the person before me is the most important deed.

If I approach each encounter with a brother or sister very much aware of the invaluable gift of the present moment, then I will strive to give my all in loving service. I will truly empty myself in loving concern for the friend I am now privileged to have at my side, for the prisoner I am now chatting with through the cell bars, for the dying mother I am now bending over to anoint, for the priest desperately seeking counsel after suffering repeated defeats with alcoholism, for the parents of the young girl tragically killed on her college campus by an unknown assailant just a few hours ago.

These are without a doubt the perfect times for me as a priest to love as Jesus has urged me to love. The perfect deed will be revealed by the genuineness of my concern. Even though I have heard repeatedly the problems that afflict all men and women, the concerns of the person now before me are unique. My own willingness to listen patiently, to give of my time and energy beyond measure, will reveal in a most real way the spirit of the Good News. I will strive to convey Jesus' love as He has loved me. My desire to be a servant in the Spirit of Jesus will sanctify the present encounter. The power of Jesus will radiate through my thoughts, my words, my deeds.

3

Christ Born in Us

More than thirty years ago, about two weeks before Christmas, our Scripture professor came to class prepared to give us a quick quiz on the events surrounding Jesus' birth as narrated in the Gospels of Luke and Matthew. These Gospels go into detail about the birth of Jesus. The Biblical account of Jesus' birth is probably the first story I ever heard. I certainly thought I was familiar with all the minute details of this event, which has had such a lasting impact on the world to this very day.

See how you fare answering the questions asked by the Scripture professor about an event we all feel so familiar with in our Christian heritage.

1. What did Mary ride on the road to Bethlehem?
2. How soon after Mary and Joseph reached Bethlehem was Jesus born?
3. What sort of building was Jesus born in?
4. What animals were gathered about the manger?
5. How many Wise Men were there?
6. How did the star compare in brightness with the other stars?
7. Who else besides the Wise Men witnessed the star?
8. Did Joseph meet the Wise Men?

These are not profound questions. I had very quick answers to all but a few. The fact is that neither Luke nor Matthew, nor, for that matter, either of the other two Gospels has answers to these questions. If you doubt this statement read Luke 2:1-20 and Matthew 2:1-23.

I thought for sure I knew the story of Jesus' birth backwards and forwards. I quickly found out I knew it backwards in that my understanding of the first Christmas has come from paintings, crib scenes, stories and Christmas cards that have appeared during the course of the last two thousand years.

There is surely nothing wrong with the traditions that have evolved around the Gospel accounts of Jesus' birth. But we must not lose sight of the *core* meaning of the biblical message. God so loved the world that He sent His only begotten Son into our midst that we, the sons and daughters of God, might have life more abundantly.

The Almighty could have chosen many and varied ways to reveal His personal love for you and me. In the Old Testament, God shared His loving concern for His chosen people time and time again. Angels disguised as men were sent by God to assure His people of His provident care. He caused armies to be brought to their knees as He protected His chosen people. God went before His people as a pillar of fire at night and a cloud during the day as they journeyed through the desert from Egypt to Israel. God continued to confirm His love and concern for the good of His chosen people by speaking through the prophets.

However, in the birth of Jesus, His taking on of our human condition, His life lived among us, His passion and death on the cross, God chose a way to reveal His personal union with all men and women. Two thousand years from the first Christmas night you and I can stand in awe before the event of His birth. We come to an even greater appreciation of God's love for us. The Son of God so humbled himself as to take upon himself our human condition. We witness Jesus in His public ministry as a compassionate, merciful, forgiving person. He mirrors the image of His Father. In death He reveals the greatest expression of His commitment to us in giving His life as a lasting testimony of His love. The Psalmist said that man is little less than an angel. I wonder! Jesus did not come as an angel. He took upon himself our humanity, except for sin. Our human condition has been exalted by Jesus.

Armies have been brought to defeat. Worldly powers have conquered lands only to fade away into oblivion. The Church has suffered persecution from without, scandal from within. When all is said and done, one truth remains: Jesus' mandate given to His apostles to "Love one another as I have loved you." This utterance of Jesus has encouraged countless men and women in every age to follow in His footsteps, has invested you and me with the power *this day* to love all in His name.

In this spirit I approach the Holy Night of Jesus' birth. I desire to live now, not I, but to let Jesus live in me.

Jesus willingly accepted His role as a servant. He was surely on no ego trip. In my own life I must continually separate my own tendency to seek recognition, influence, even power, for the reality in faith that I have been called to be a servant in the likeness of my Master.

I observe in the Gospels Jesus' desire to be with His own. There was no attempt on His part to have a ministry by remote control. I can't for one moment imagine that Jesus would have let red tape, administrative matters, form letters, committees, or whatever would have been their conterpart in His time, to come between Him and the people He had come to serve: the suffering, the lonely, the sick, the rejected, the hungry, the frightened, the sinful. He moved among His own, those in dire need of His healing touch.

I can so easily overlook the obvious, the servant posture my Savior so willingly adopted. I am called to be another Christ. The sick in mind and heart, the lonely, the rejected, the sinful, the people He served — they are still present in my day. It is my sublime task to seek them out in His name. "I have not come to be served but to serve."

I simply must ask myself, am I willing to pay the price of discipleship? My commitment to Jesus will continually upset the routine, the status quo, of my life. His Spirit will not let me settle for mediocrity in my calling but will urge me on to greatness. Each day will present new challenges to put on His mind and heart. He asks me to embrace the indifferent, the suffering, the rejected, the poor of my people, those I often find difficult to give my time and effort to. They are precious in His eyes. They are created in the image and likeness of God. All this will demand of me acceptance of His lifestyle, His values, His attitudes. This is truly a lifetime task. I pray fervently to measure up to His call.

I pray with my people that Jesus will enter our lives even at the risk of changing them. Together we can seek out the lost and bring new hope; together we can heal the broken in heart so they can again see purpose in their lives; together we can feed the hungry to enable them to witness more clearly eternal values at work in us; together we can free the guilt-ridden by gracious forgiveness and wholehearted acceptance; together we can bring peace and comfort by our sensitivity to the needs of the less fortunate; together we can rebuild our own community so we seek first the kingdom of God.

This is the reality of Jesus in our midst. Only when I and my people are deeply convinced of this truth can we say together that we are living the Spirit, the mission, the message of Jesus. We must have Jesus born anew into our hearts every day.

In Bethlehem, Christmas hymns are sung year-round. It is a powerful reminder to every pilgrim visiting the place of Jesus' birth that the spirit of Christmas, the love it so tenderly reveals, must be lived year-round.

There is no other season of the year that means more to me than Advent and Christmas. The four weeks of anticipation, the reflective mood of Midnight Mass when you actually see the stars in children's eyes, and tears of gratitude in the eyes of parents and grandparents, the opportunity of being more thoughtful to others, the loving spirit that seems to permeate all, the smell of spices, the roast turkey with all the familiar trimmings, the varied Christmas trees and packages surrounding them — all are precious happenings. I always whisper a silent prayer of gratitude for having witnessed another Christmas.

With all the joy of anticipation, the familiar happenings of the season, I must admit at times to mixed emotions. I want to enjoy the days to the full, capture each moment for happy memories; but there is a haunting thought that creeps into my heart even in the midst of all that goes to make the season so beautiful.

I think of the blind girl who once told me that the Christmas holidays are the most difficult days of the year. So many visitors, so many expressions of love, treats galore — all to disappear in such a short time. Then she is left alone with her memories to suffer the pangs of loneliness. Throughout the year she needs visitors who are ever conscious of what it means to be in an institution, to be blind for a lifetime.

I call to mind the poor family literally surrounded with Christmas packages containing foods they enjoy but once a year. Throughout the rest of the year they make their way to our local Division of Family Services where they fill out detailed forms, endure long waits, before they are able to pick up government-surplus commodities. The poor need sustaining sensitivity to their predicament the year round.

My thoughts go to the penitent seeking forgiveness on Christmas Eve. I know that lasting peace of mind and heart will be found only by the Christian who seeks daily to live in the presence of Jesus. The graces of the Sacrament of Reconciliation can vanish so quickly if we fail to work for a new beginning. Just to feel relieved at Christmas is not enough for a strong faith life. We can so easily return to our own little world of self-centeredness, unaware of the hidden greatness of the Spirit wanting to work within us.

I give generously at Christmas but I cannot help but think of all those occasions throughout the year when, often due to a lack of thoughtfulness, I miss those opportunities to place a few dollars in the hands of people who are in dire need. The poor, the rejected, are with me always. I must seek them out and know it is a privilege to give. What I have beyond my reasonable needs belongs to the poor.

My thoughts are especially with a middle-aged couple whose son took his life the summer before. This will be their first Christmas without his presence. They struggled for ten years with their son as alcohol continued to make deeper inroads in his life. When he was placed to rest his father told me. "Now I can visit my son knowing he can no longer run away." We will visit his grave during the holidays. I will whisper a prayer of hope and call to mind those young men and women still among the living who are caught up in the shackles of alcohol and drug abuse.

Such example can arouse noble feelings within myself. They will mean very little if I fail in a real way to understand the misery, the hurt feelings, the sufferings of those around me. Surely sentiment, even a tinge of sadness, is valid during the Christmas season. These examples serve as a timely warning for me not to merely weep over human sufferings, but to challenge the evil that causes them.

At Christmas time, most of us are frantically trying to think of gifts for all those special people on our shopping lists. We want gifts that are original, are meaningful, and fit our budget. Here's a list of gift suggestions for the large of heart and small of purse. These gifts won't cost you a dime, but that does not mean they have no value. On the contrary, when you give one of these gifts, you are giving the most priceless gift of all: yourself.

The gift of forgiveness. Doctors tell us that many of our physical ills are directly attributable to an unforgiving heart. When we are burdened with hurt and bitterness toward another person, the stress and anxiety accompanying this sad condition wreak havoc on our physical being. We are admonished by the Word of God not even to approach the altar without first making peace with our neighbor. This is the time to heal the wounds of the past. Christmas is a good time to take the first step in bringing about a spirit of reconciliation between ourselves and someone we have hurt or someone who has hurt us. We can take this step by sending a thoughtful card, by calling or visiting in a forgiving spirit. This demands bigness of heart — spiritual maturity. We must forgive as we have so often been forgiven by our God and by our neighbor.

The gift of listening. We can reveal the warmth of friendship by being present to another who is very much alone in this world. During the holidays people will flock into nursing homes, mental hospitals, homes for "homeless" boys and girls, bringing baskets of food and much good cheer. However, the gift of listening demands more than a one-time visit at Christmas. Listening is an enduring quality. When the festive lights and decorations are put away for another year, are we still ready to give of our time in listening, in being present to someone precious in the eyes of the Lord? The face before us is made in the image of God. The fidgety and slouching body confronting us in the nursing home is a temple of the Spirit. We are constantly amazed at what God has wrought. Our gift of self is a gift to the Body of Christ.

The gift of prayer. There is no greater spiritual gift than to lift others up in prayer. Clement of Alexandria called prayer "keeping company with God." Keeping company involves gesture and silence, relaxed reflection and intent speaking. In this spirit we can remember frequently those we hold close and those who have entered our lives this very day. The parishioner hurting in mind and body because she has an alcoholic husband who refuses to face the problem *believes* that my prayers and remembrance of him at Mass will make a difference. Recently, I met a very frightened lady who was being admitted to the hospital for surgery. She asked for my prayers. I could sense her anguish, and promised to remember her that very day in my prayers —a privilege, a sacred promise. What seems a hopeless cause begins to work out in God's time. What is confusing begins to reveal purpose. We begin to see, even in tragedy, the hand of God. Above all, we become more aware of God's presence in the small and great of our daily lives. All this we lift up to God as we pray for our brothers and sisters. We are convinced of the grace-full *power* found in prayer.

The gift of love expressed. The gift of love can be expressed in a thousand ways every day. Love *is* the universal language. Scripture says "Faith, hope and love — and the greatest of these is love." Take the precious time to tell your wife or husband, your children, your mother and father that you love them. A tender kiss of appreciation, the warmth of an embrace for a task well done, a pat on the back or the gentle squeeze of the hand reveals the depth of our sensitivity. A greeting card sent with a note of appreciation written at the bottom instead of just the customary signature will do much to express a true spirit of concern. Now is the appointed time. It is our commitment in life to love *now* as Jesus loves us.

Some Reflections on Jesus' Birth
Some seven hundred and fifty years ago, St. Francis of Assisi knelt before the crib scene he had fashioned with his own hands. The birth of Jesus came vividly alive to Francis and his followers as they recalled the events of the first Holy Night.

With all the customary preparations for the commemoration of Jesus' birth — the liturgy to be readied, the confessions to be heard, the remembrance of people I hold so dear, the wrapping of gifts, the mailing of cards — I must steal time to reflect on the profound truths of the Holy Night we celebrate.

As I reflect on that first Holy Night, I picture in my mind the entire scene of Jesus' birth. The stable where Jesus was born was never meant to be His home. It was all that was available to Mary and Joseph. This alone causes me to reflect on our home. I pray it will always be a place of hospitality to everyone who comes to our door. In each I will strive to see the image of Jesus. I will open our door graciously not only to those who bring warmth into our home but to those who have been hurt, who feel distant even in the midst of my loving concern. I pray for the gift of hospitality.

As I visualize the star that gave direction to the Magi I pray to be an instrument of guidance to those who seek my help. May my words come from conviction. May the example of my life be in tune with my words. I must urge my brothers to seek first the kingdom of God. My inner peace and fulfillment of my brother priests will be found only in the heart of our calling to be servants like unto our Master. If my interests are centered elsewhere I will lose the spirit of my calling, and my priesthood will become a job to be fulfilled but lacking spirit and life. I pray for myself and for my brother priests — for singleness of purpose to be other Christs in our time.

The magi were God-fearing men. They were deeply convinced of God's presence in this world. I pray for their faith as I look out upon the world, where there are numerous wars being fought. In all this I try to see God's redemptive grace. Even as wars go on there are countless people performing great acts of charity to alleviate pain, to bring hope to the lonely heart, to feed the hungry, to bring a new tomorrow to many. This is God's redemptive grace working in a world so much at odds with itself. I pray to appreciate God's presence in the midst of contradictions.

The shepherds in the fields that first Holy Night were common folk. They were not puffed up with their self-importance. The angels announced the good news of Jesus' birth to the shepherds, so I must never forget that God calls the least among us to tasks of great glory. Some of my brother priests received great recognition while many others live, faithfully serve and die almost unnoticed. How many miracles of grace have been revealed through these unheralded servants? No matter how hidden away a priest's work may seem after years of service, his hands have ministered life unto many. I pray I will appreciate the goodness of my God revealed in those who quietly serve. May I have faith, the humility of Joseph. He wondered, then obeyed when he could not understand. I pray often for a more profound faith and still find myself dearly wanting certitude. Although Joseph seemed to remain very much in the background, he moved ahead with singleness of purpose, seeking only to do God's will in loving concern for Mary and their Son. I pray again this day that I will continue in my faith and loving concern for those I am called to serve.

Mary, in the presence of the angel, hesitated for a few moments before she spoke those immortal words, "Be it done unto me according to your word." She then surrendered herself into God's hands! When she visited her cousin Elizabeth some time later, she could say with joyful humility, "My soul does magnify the Lord — He has done great things in me." Only when I surrender myself into His hands can He do great things in me. I pray for this complete surrender, knowing that, no matter how insignificant I may feel, God can do great things in me! This is the self-worth of every Christian who is ready to spend himself and be spent in the service of his brothers and sisters. What a tremendous calling ours is!

4

The Gift of Friendship

Often I have gone to other people, seeking their help for those in need. The most distressing response I have heard is, "Father, I do not want to get involved." For some it may be the scar of past times when they gave and their attempt to reach out was rejected. Others are doing their own thing comfortably. To become involved intimately in the lives of others, where real needs exist, would be a risk to their contentment. Whatever the reason, the failure to become involved in the struggles and triumphs of our brothers and sisters can spell death to any real growth in the Spirit. We settle for mediocrity rather than greatness in our calling to the second-greatest commandment, "Love your neighbor as yourself."

We need each other to walk in the Spirit of Jesus, to draw others to the saving mission of Jesus, to die in the fullness of our belief in Jesus who triumphed over death.

A Christian who believes he can walk in the footsteps of the Master without assistance from his brothers and sisters is living in delusion. If he does not come to the realization of his need for others, he will thwart the unlimited potential to love, which is born in those created to the image and likeness of God. "For if either of them falls, the one will lift up his companion. But woe to the one who falls when there is not another to lift him up" (Ecclesiastes).

The calling of a Christian is not to live in isolation but to share the joys of Christian living with all those he meets in his daily life —not just with his family, his co-workers, and his friends, but with the rejected, the hurt, those suffering in mind and heart, the poor, the imprisoned. Only when you and I become absorbed in the mission of Jesus as participants relating to, sharing with and caring for others in His name will we experience the fullness of our calling as Christians. This is authentic Christianity. In the early Church, nonbelievers were attracted to the Christian community when they witnessed first-hand how the Christians loved one another.

A few years after my ordination, I joined a group of five other priests who met every two weeks to share their desire to live more fully a life in the spirit of our calling. Although we knew for a fact that our gatherings would foster greater dedication in our various ministries, our prime goal was to grow in closer union with one another and thereby share more intimately our common desire to put on the mind and heart of our Master.

We had spent many years together in the seminary but had little intimate understanding of one another's longings, hopes, fears and dreams. Such a spirit of intimacy was not encouraged in our formative years. We were brought together in community but our relationships often remained on a very superficial level. Such relationships did not permit pulling back the mask, revealing one's inner self.

Our first meeting—possibly even the second gathering of this small group of priests—proved a bit awkward for all. It was an entirely new experience. We had to learn how to speak with one another in a loving, concerned and revealing manner. It was not long, though, before a dynamic change took place in the group. We quickly became conscious of the workings of the Spirit among us. We recognized through the intimacy of honest communication how distinct each one present was but, at the same time, how we needed each other to complement and fulfill the tremendous potential abiding in the heart of each one of us. The small group became one in the uniqueness of our calling. As we were able to share intimately with one another, we were able to share more intimately with God. It calls to mind the words of St. Teresa of Avila: "Mental prayer in my opinion is nothing else than an intimate sharing between friends; it means taking time frequently to be alone with God who we know loves us."

When these gatherings would come to an end I would go to my room to jot down new insights revealed by my brother priests, ways of coping with problems common to all of us, inspiring comments. Often, profound thoughts had been expressed by those I had taken for granted. I had been totally unaware of their inner selves, the reflection of God's goodness in them.

One of the greatest things a Christian can do is share in building up a community. For our own peace of mind, for our growth together in the Spirit of Jesus, we cannot live together as marbles in a bag, with everyone doing his own thing, unconcerned, indifferent to the needs of brother and sister. Such an approach eats away at the whole concept of Christian commitment.

Building up community in any form demands an openness of mind and heart by all members, a willingness to share, to trust. We know from experience how fragile we are — how easily shattered if our relationships with others prove uncaring, indifferent, superficial. This is the risk we take if we are determined to love as Jesus loves. The rewards of such a Christ-centered approach far outweigh the risks.

Growing in intimacy with one another will of necessity demand a sharing of our time, often putting aside plans, anticipating the needs of others, being ever open to sharing our experiences as fellow pilgrims. Often, in times of personal tragedy it will be more important just to remain silent — only our presence need be felt.

Friendship is a priceless gift. The love of another person cannot be bought. It must be freely given, freely accepted. And, above all, friendship is not an overnight accomplishment but a gift to be nurtured with an ever deepening sense of commitment. This love is possible because I have been created to the image and likeness of God. I can freely love another as God loves me.

Friendship comes into existence in freedom, continues to grow in respect for one another's freedom and endures for the long haul by the give-and-take demanded by each new day, by listening, by sharing strengths and weaknesses. True friendship never becomes stagnant. It is a movement, a boundless adventure that at times places heavy demands on my time, my energy, my very self, but then I begin to experience what it means to love in this life as I will someday love in the next. It is worth the personal cost.

As *The Imitation of Christ* mentions, I am able to have but a few intimate friends. However, the love I have for them, if it is to be true and enduring, is the love I want to share with all who cross my path in life. It is not possible to love all in the same degree but I am called to love all in the same spirit. Sharing my joys and sorrows, my dreams and my frustrations, my successes and my failures with my friends makes me ever more sensitive to all who enter my life. I can share wholeheartedly in the good fortune of another. I can be there to pick up the pieces when a dream comes tumbling down.

There are those who make a distinction between acquaintances and friends: an acquaintance is someone who enters our life in no significant way. People, no matter how briefly they enter my life, are too precious for such a distinction to be made. As a Christian, as one who has experienced the warmth, the gift of friendship, I want to reveal my desire to love all men and women: the waitress, the bank teller, the young man pumping gas, the bus driver, the penitent, my bishop, the neighbor next door, my brother priests, the Servants. I love them in the Spirit of Jesus, in the spirit of friendship. The person before me now deserves my love and full attention. How powerful is a simple expression of love and concern to someone you may never meet again.

In quiet times it is good to reflect on those gifts that inspire us to live life more fully. The gift of friendship brings out the very best in me and brings good to many others. What is from God cannot be locked up within. It must be shared with all.

Words and actions not expressed have a tendency to wither, to die on the vine. Expressing genuine affection for those who enter our lives has a return value far beyond price, and often beyond our awareness. "It is in giving that we too receive." People are drawn to a person who is sensitive and acts upon that sensitivity. The warmth of love is contagious. If I am determined to love beyond measure, the love I so generously give will spread to others like one candle being lit by another.

You are a lovable person. Yes, you and I each have an Achilles heel; chinks in our armor often reveal themselves. But if we look beyond the human condition there is good to be found in all of us. That good must be discovered and praised. Some criticism may help us to grow in sensitivity to one another's needs — but too much is a subtle poison.

You and I desire above all else to love and be loved. It is as basic to our human nature — being created to the image and likeness of God—as breathing. The desire to love, to see the good in our neighbor, is surely present, but we sorely miss the spirit of Jesus' command when we fail to express our inner sentiments in words and actions. This is our precious time to express daily our love, our appreciation for all those who enter our lives. This is the way to stay in love with the wonder of life.

5

A Time for Prayer

As a priest, I often wonder if I am truly convinced of the absolute necessity of striving daily for a deeper, more intense life in the Spirit. There is probably no other profession in the world wherein a person can achieve his goal (ordination) one day, receive the respect of so many, and yet never be required to open another book the rest of his life. As we priests know, it is easy to settle for mediocrity in our calling no matter how objectively profound our priestly vocation is viewed in theological discourses or in the minds and hearts of our people.

Gabriel Marcel, the French philosopher who died a few years ago, once made a statement I'll never forget. "Many people who say they believe, do not believe. Many people who say they do not believe, by their actions reveal they do believe." I wonder if these words at times apply to me. I can speak glibly of eternal truths and yet by my actions cause people to wonder if my words, my deeds, are the product of any real intimacy with God in prayer, from a consciousness of His presence in my life.

To become a priest I made sacrifices. I freely chose to walk in the footsteps of the Master, which is surely no easy task. After making such a choice it seems foolhardy to run the course in any halfway fashion. By falling into a rut of daily living, I can so easily negate the tremendous good that God can do in me. I can even convince myself I'm doing a great job and yet waste so much precious time because I lack any real depth in my relationship with my God. I can go through the externals in grand style but fail to reveal the greatness of my calling in any meaningful, lasting way.

The interior life is above all a life of intimacy with God who lives in me. I am called to open the floodgates of His love in devoted service.

To seek a more intimate relation with God, to strengthen my faith in those things that must come first in my life, is not an easy task. An

appreciation for moments of silence and solitude is a spiritual conquest not easily won. It takes daily persevering effort on my part.
However, the reward is great: I begin to taste the sweetness of the
Lord. The daily ministrations of my priesthood take on real meaning. I
live in His presence.

I am called to be a man of prayer. In faith I know that nothing
meaningful or lasting can be accomplished without a profound
appreciation of the need for prayer, the lifting of my mind and heart to
my God. In daily prayer I simply ask God for the enlightenment to see
myself for what I am so I might make the honest effort to become what
I ought to be. As a priest I do this in the Spirit of Jesus as He spoke to
His Father the night before He was to endure His passion and death:
"Father, for them do I sanctify myself." There are risks to be encoun-
tered in honest prayer. Changes will be demanded the more determined
I am to walk in His footsteps. I will experience within myself more and
more divine discontent with the old man. I will make the necessary
changes not only for my spiritual good but for the good of those I am
called to serve. Father, for them — my people — do I sanctify myself.

The opportunities for personal sacrifice will be many. What I
dare to dream I must dare to do. Simple things like graciously inter-
rupting an interesting TV program to speak to someone in the parlor;
answering the phone late at night for a call that could have been made
earlier in the day; the change of vacation plans due to the illness of a
brother priest; the long ride to comfort the sick; the schedules broken
for the unexpected; giving of my little extra to someone in real need;
my willingness to stay with someone for the long haul even though my
efforts so often seem in vain; my willingness to endure hurt and
disappointment when my best efforts to assist come to nought. Daily
experiences like these demand a constant spirit of self-discipline. It is
so easy for me to delude myself by scheduling my day around my own
likes and dislikes. My concern should center around the unpredictable
needs of people this day.

I have personally found that the vitality of my inner life goes up or
down in proportion to how faithful I am to daily reading of Holy
Scripture, reading inspiring books or listening to inspirational tapes.

All three help me be open to the Spirit, keep me in close contact with the true values of life, and, above all, urge me on to live my priesthood more abundantly. They open the door to His power within me. The energy, endurance, courage and capacity that so often remain dormant within me begin to rise. I find myself literally pushed on to greater resolves. "I can do all things through Christ who gives me the strength." My sermons, my confessional admonitions, my writings, my visits to the jail, my consoling of the sick, my willingness to give more fully of myself reflect my faithfulness to those moments I set aside each day for the Word.

Through daily spiritual reading I have had the grace to walk among the great. The more I honestly admit to my human condition, the more I desire to seek out through reading those who have fought the good battle, have lived in witness of Jesus and have won the crown. I am inspired by their words. I am urged on to use my allotted time in loving service. For me, living out the mission of Jesus is impossible without the habitual vision of greatness.

As a priest I have been given the privilege of arranging my daily schedule with more flexibility of time than any other profession I am aware of. I pray each day to be ever conscious of the sanctity of each moment. Precious moments can slip through my hands like sand through an hourglass, never to be retrieved. So much time can be wasted in slow beginnings and in low-quality performance. I am at this time in my earthly sojourn vividly aware of this fact as the precious gift of eyesight I have so long taken for granted becomes uncertain.

Treasure the time set aside for the written word. There are few endeavors more important for the growth of the kingdom of Jesus from within than one's choice of reading. Out of the hidden springs, the rivers of life rise. Only when my spoken word, my written word, and my actions reveal that the kingdom of God comes first in my life can I ever hope to assist my brothers and sisters to think as Jesus would think, to speak as Jesus would speak, to act as Jesus would act.

It is so easy for me to jump on the treadmill of daily activity and to put aside what is so essential to the inner life of my calling as a

Christian. I can excuse myself from prayer, from spiritual reading, so I can be always available to my people. The truth is, the spring of my inner life in the Spirit will soon go dry. Always being available without taking time to rekindle the Spirit may actually result in a disservice. We can live in busy superficiality with little depth of conviction. I can quickly become a spiritual caterer going through the fiery hoop each day, professing my belief but lacking spirit and life. What a waste! I am called to greatness of spirit.

Jesus often went apart from His disciples and from the people He had come to serve. He would then return renewed in spirit. The Christian who resolves to go apart to deepen his life in the Spirit will be a giant.

The Cure' of Ars once noticed an old farmer who came to his parish church every day to kneel before the Blessed Sacrament. The farmer had no beads in hand, no prayer book to read. The Cure' was curious. He asked the farmer how he prayed. The answer was profound: "He looks at me. I look at Him." Sometimes I feel my prayer life is directed to many particular intentions and I lose hold of the wonder of surrender in prayer. Christian prayer is not some magical experience to control my Creator. It is a loving communion with Him. In silence His love is revealed, His will made clear. Many words are not needed. He knows my desire to serve. He knows full well the roadblocks I often place in my path, thwarting the full accomplishment of His will in me. As I look at Him, as He looks at me, truth is revealed. The grace to move on in His Spirit is again revealed.

Persistence in prayer is needed not to bend God's will to mine, but to bend my will to His. In persevering prayer I find ways of opening my life to the goodness of my God, to a greater appreciation of myself as a wonder of His creation and of my neighbor created in His image. Above all, I am again made conscious of those values that must come first in my life if precious time is not to be wasted. It is so easy to be busy about many things that appear—or I stamp to be — God-centered. Often the busy-ness is just an excuse to avoid confrontation with my God in silent prayer. The truth revealed in silence often upsets my established priorities. The haunting words of Leon Bloy come to mind: "The only sorrow is not to be a saint!" The sad truth is that I can avoid becoming a saint because I am busy about many other things, seemingly so important, with many pious desires but little effort made at fulfillment. I cheat myself and those I serve. Prayer makes visible God's will and also reveals what in my life is hampering the fulfillment of His will. Prayer forces me to face the reality of life stripped to its essentials. It reveals how weak and limited I am and that without Him I can do nothing. I must, regardless of personal cost, live the truth discovered when I confront my God in honest prayer.

Prayer brings light to my hopes, to my aspirations. It enables me to discover my true desires and goals, so easily forgotten in the hustle and bustle of daily living. Prayer is for me an act of cleansing. It gives me the repeated opportunity of being honest with my God, with myself and with my neighbor.

Spirit of Light, imprint upon my mind, in characters that can never be erased, this truth: that my apostolate will be successful only in the measure that I live that supernatural inner life of which you are the sovereign Principle and Jesus Christ the Source.

In my desire to truly walk more fully in the footsteps of my Lord I find it vitally important to make a consistent effort to do things for the right reasons. This sounds like a self-evident truth, but it is a difficult truth for me to live out. To achieve purity of intention is a lifelong endeavor. It is necessary for me to sift out what is true and authentic from what is false and unauthentic in order to walk in the footsteps of my Lord. Therein lies the cost of discipleship.

Prayer is the opening of my mind and heart to my Lord. When I fail to seek quiet times for prayer, my own agenda of imagined self-importance and my desire to look good quickly enter the picture. The minimum requirement for candles used at the altar is that they contain at least fifty-one percent beeswax. Similarly, when prayer takes a second place in my life, I find myself content just meeting the minimum requirement. I find myself doing good things — even sublime things — for about fifty-one percent the right reasons.

At these times I thank God for the Spirit of Light. I am urged by the Spirit to get out of the fast lane and seek quiet times to renew my relationship with my Lord. In these quiet times I am again brought to the realization that my Lord is not only to be my Director but also my Audience. All things are to be done through Him, with Him, in Him and for Him.

I sorely need these times apart so I can again focus on my Lord in all I think, do and say. I am called to holiness in my daily life. The measure of the good that the Lord will accomplish in me will be in direct proportion to my own willingness to put aside the things of this world and seek first and always the kingdom of my Lord. I desire to be holy — a priest on fire with love for his Lord and those created to His image. This determination of mind and heart will set others on fire so they too can taste the sweetness of the Lord. Goodness inspires goodness.

Life in the Spirit is nourished in me by the reality of my own relationship with my Lord in prayer. My Lord becomes the center, the reason, the motivation, the direction and the purpose of my life. This attitude of mind and heart will only be attained when I directly confront my motives in the presence of my Lord.

In quiet times I am able to put aside self-conceived answers, remove prejudices, sort out mixed feelings and seek the reality of my Lord's vision for me. When I fail to do this, I make poor judgments. I misread the actions of others. I store up feelings of resentment.

There is no more important aspect of my quest for holiness than a genuine openness of mind and heart to my Lord in prayer. In order for my prayer life to be effective in clearing my vision, it must be completely sincere. This means stripping off all masks, all vestiges of sham and pretense. Rationalization and excuses must go. My prayer life will then be an honest communication with my Lord of how I feel in good times, in bad times. As with a friend, my relationship with my Lord depends upon a full and open sharing of my thoughts and feelings.

May I be a healing grace in the lives of others. May my joy and peace be a leaven to all I meet. May I readily admit when the path becomes crooked in my own life. May I join hands with all my brothers and sisters in good times and in bad. May I be the Christ-like witness I am called to be.

A few months ago I heard a prominent evangelist make the statement that he was sick and tired of dead preachers giving dead sermons to dead congregations. I am sure this rather harsh statement was an overreaction to some disappointing experiences with Sunday worship services. Attending an uninspired Sunday Mass along with a poorly prepared sermon presents a stumbling block to meaningful worship and even more so to the deepening of one's faith life.

Many religious writers are convinced that much indifference among the faithful is the direct result of stagnant worship. Dead worship produces dying Christians.

A circuit judge told me the other day he often finds himself thinking out a problem case during Sunday Mass. "Everything is routine and the sermons often ill-prepared." So often this is true. I knew of a priest who each week worked diligently on his sermon, consulting many and varied books offering homily suggestions, polishing and refining his composition until it was letter-perfect. Still, his congregation did not respond to his sermons. In preparing a sermon it is necessary to spend quiet time in prayer in order to become tuned in to the everyday needs of our people. We beg for the grace to approach them with a compassionate heart that will inspire them to rise from mediocrity of spirit to greatness of spirit.

We, the priests and the people of God, are to be joint participants and not mere observers at Sunday Mass. If we are truly believers, the time given to worship on Sunday is treasured time. Worship of our God, our Father, is the primary work of the Church. All else — teaching, serving one another in charity, mission endeavors —follows from our conviction that there is an all-loving God, deserving of our worship in private and together in the family of God.

We priests, the leaders of Israel, are called upon to do all in our power to bring spirit and life to Sunday worship. We can unconsciously become very matter-of-fact in saying Mass, evidencing little conviction in what we are about. On the other hand, our sermons can begin with the fervent faith we reveal as we genuflect before His real presence in the tabernacle; as we kiss the altar, calling to mind those who have died so faithfully in His service; as we read the words of Jesus; as we pray fervently for those in need; as we offer the bread and wine to become His body and blood for all to adore; as we join with our people in saying the prayer He himself first said; as we reverently place the body of Jesus in the hands of the faithful and as we finally beg God's blessing on all our endeavors throughout the coming week.

The real test of the genuineness of our participation in Sunday Mass will be evidenced in how we make every effort to live out the mission and message of Jesus among our brothers and sisters after we leave the church doors. Our devout attendance at Mass will enable us to become ever more open to the workings of the Spirit — wisdom, compassion, forgiveness.

The grace received at Holy Mass will help us distinguish what is of temporary worth from what is of eternal value. Then only can we seek first the kingdom of God. We will be ever more sensitive to the needs of our brothers and sisters, and will meet them where they are and not where we would like them to be. We will be quick to forgive others as we would want to be forgiven.

If we leave the church on Sunday morning with the resolution to make these things a reality in our lives, then the time set aside for Sunday observance will come alive. Sunday observance will no longer be an obligation but an opportunity to grow in the Spirit. We will look forward to the many priceless occasions during the week to reveal Jesus in our thoughts, our words, our actions.

Father Gerald Fitzgerald, founder of the Servants of the Paraclete, had a consuming devotion to the Holy Eucharist. Father Gerald provided in our constitution that all our houses would oberve times of adoration before the Blessed Sacrament. Each member of the community and our neighbors have the opportunity of spending an hour in silent prayer, spiritual reading, quiet reflection. How precious these moments of quiet are when I ask for integrity of mind and heart to be honest with my God and with myself.

While sitting in quiet reverence in front of the Western Wall (Wailing Wall) in Jerusalem, a priest friend of mine, who has lived in the Holy Land for many years, made a wise observation. He mentioned that the Jews need the Wall because it represents God's presence in their lives. Moslems hold the Dome of the Rock in Jerusalem as sacred in their belief. We Catholics have great respect for the ground that Jesus walked upon some 2000 years ago. But we really do not have an urgent need for these shrines. We are blessed abundantly with our belief in the real presence of Jesus in the Eucharist. He is present in our huge cathedrals. He is present in our small Chapel in Dittmer, Missouri. I kneel in awe before the Blessed Sacrament, believing that the same Jesus who walked through Galilee some 2000 years ago, healing the sick, giving sight to the blind, and above all, removing the burden of guilt from the sinner, the same Jesus who hung on the cross at Calvary, whose blood the soldiers trampled, is living and present.

In His presence I ask for a compassionate heart to reach out to my brothers and sisters. Many of their needs are not obvious. I pray to perceive those who feel rejected, beaten down and abandoned but who so often keep their hurt hidden within. When someone asks us how we are feeling we automatically respond, "I feel fine — nothing's wrong." It can be a mask to cover hidden fear, nagging doubts or a dread of feeling alone in the world. To paraphrase James, "It is easy to say, 'Have a nice day,' and not become involved."

I pray I will always have the courage to move from what I am comfortable and familiar with to what may be very uncomfortable in service to my brothers and sisters. This is the cost of discipleship.

The Risks of Prayer

The first risk is that of seeing myself as I truly am. What I think about myself is often what I want to be, not what I am. Genuine prayer demands that I be honest with myself. What are my motives, my dominant desires? What is my attitude toward all men? What are my weaknesses and strengths? Prayer is a beautiful, if humbling, practice. Lord, grant me the grace to see myself for what I am so I might become what I ought to be! In our dealings with God we have to come clean.

The second risk is the danger of becoming more like Christ in a world that often rejects His values. In the very beginning of Christ's ministry he rejected the temptations to use His personal power to seek worldly renown. His integrity brought Him not fame and fortune but loneliness and a felon's death. I am asked to walk in His footsteps. In prayer I am urged by the Spirit to measure up to the challenge in every aspect of my life.

The third risk in prayer is the danger of having my prayers answered. I pray for peace but it must begin with me. I pray to love my neighbor. Am I willing to go beyond convenience in my willingness to serve? I pray to be honest. But wait a minute — am I ready to give up my pretensions?

God grant me the courage to run the risks of prayer, of seeing myself as I am, the willingness to pay the cost of discipleship, of measuring up to the reality of having my prayers answered.

There is a vast difference between saying prayers and praying.

6

A Time for Silence

We live today a feverish existence, in a continual bustle. The rectory phone rings from morning to night, people are waiting in the parlor, we are submerged under piles of paperwork. There is scarcely time to take meals and still less time to stand in silence before God, and immerse ourselves in what He says to us. But if we as the leaders of Israel are to be effective channels of grace, we cannot delude ourselves into believing this is possible without time for silent prayer. It has been said that God speaks to us in a whisper, and it is only in silent prayer that we are able to hear Him.

Gabriel Marcel once stated that our generation fears silence. You see a young boy walking down the street with a pocket radio to his ear. Background music is the in thing in our business establishments. I find myself with the TV on even though I do not have the slightest notion what is going on; in some way it provides company. I saw a jogger the other day running along the road with earphones connected to a small radio on his belt. There is surely nothing wrong with any of these experiences. However, I fear that I can easily be robbed of the silence, the times of quiet, the solitude.

I see the need to literally steal time for silence. Very often I would rather fill my time with the immediate concerns of the day. This I can often handle better than silence. I find myself like the hamster on a treadmill: constantly going but often failing to arrive at a meaningful conclusion to the activity at hand.

After I finally seek out time for silent reflection, I readily see how precious these moments are for the very heart of my calling to be another Christ.

Solitude gives me the opportunity to simply listen to my Master. I am in constant need of healing. In silence Jesus can take control. I place my utter trust in Him. "I am the way, the truth, the life." I desire with all my heart for His Spirit to dwell in me. I am not here to straighten out others. I am here so Jesus can prepare His way in me. I find it difficult, painful at times to accept quiet times; but once entered, I never regret a moment of the time I spend in listening. He brings me face to face with the realities of life. In real stillness much is revealed. Solitude is a spiritual conquest not easily won. Silent prayer demands sincere and persevering effort. It is much easier to wrap myself up in externals — even the externals of religious belief — and live on the surface. In silence I taste the sweetness of the Lord. In silence my convictions become a living part of my very being. Then, and then alone, can I reveal to others the depth of my faith, the strength of my hope in things to come, the staying-power of my charity.

It is also in silence that I find myself becoming increasingly conscious of the needs of those I am called to serve, growing ever more sensitive to them. I fool myself and waste precious time if I think holiness can be achieved in any other way. In silence I earnestly pray to rise from mediocrity and to be shown the way in my priestly calling.

We have all heard words spoken in a split second that were so meaningful they became engraved in our minds, never to be forgotten. Over thirty years ago a retreat master made a statement I am sure will remain with me till the day I die: "If we would spend twice as much time on the contemplative aspect of our calling, we would quickly find we would accomplish twice as much in the active ministry in half as much time." In other words, if I am a man of prayer — if I am a man who treasures moments of silence — then I will speak, act and think from a strong faith rooted in my love for my God and for my people created in His image.

Interior silence, prayer, will bring forth the spirit and life I need to move mountains, to reach out to my brothers and sisters. My words will ring with depth of conviction. My life will reveal singleness of purpose. Those who are lukewarm will be inspired to move from darkness to light when they observe the inner peace in my life. Those who have zeroed in on themselves will discover that it is in giving that they too will receive. They will break the chain of selfishness and joyfully give of themselves in loving service. They will begin to understand how blessed it is to love. They will be able to endure persecution from without and conflict from within, because they will be believers not only in word but in deed. They will seek the kingdom of God before all else. They will, by the grace of God, the power of prayer and the strength of good example, willingly accept the sacrifices demanded by discipleship.

This may seem unattainable. No, it is not. It is at the heart of Christian commitment. If I fail to strive daily to make my Christian commitment real in every aspect of my life, I am selling myself short. I am choosing an easy Gospel that will bury me in mediocrity and allow my people to fall into indifference, living life on the surface. My faith will become an empty symbol having lost spirit and life.

To be a man of God I must willingly accept the challenge of silent prayer, of an inner life that will daily strengthen my faith in a loving God and strengthen my belief in my brothers and sisters as temples of the Spirit. My people will cease to become an index of names, a row of faces I see on Sunday mornings. I will see each individual as a temple of the Spirit in which Jesus lives or desires to live. I will have new eyes to see all my brothers and sisters as building stones in the city of God, each unique unto themselves with a given goal, a mission to be performed, a vocation to be lived.

There are many new visions in the Church this day. We are concerned with a more meaningful liturgy, the role of the people of God in the Church, bishops working in closer union with our Holy Father, the Church and the world of today and many other exciting ideas. So many noble pursuits, but — the basic fact remains as true today as it did two thousand years ago — holiness of life in imitation of the Master is the rock-bottom answer to a vital Christianity. Jesus spent the first thirty years of His life in seclusion. He went into the desert for forty days before beginning His ministry. He often went to the mountain to be apart from His people — to commune with His God. And finally He sought silence in the Garden of Olives on the night before He was crucified.

I do not want to be under any delusion. My Christian endeavors — in particular my mission as a Servant of the Paraclete among my brother priests — demands holiness in purpose and action. What a tragedy when even the most noble Christian endeavor becomes self-serving and fails to serve the needs of my people. In silence I come face to face with my God, a God who can neither deceive nor be deceived. I come back to the fountainhead in order to see better where I am going, where I ought to go and beg for the faith, the courage, to stay on course. I am deeply convinced that if I fail to seek my God in silence I will never bring about anything worthwhile in those things I can feel, see and touch, or in the spoken word. Silent prayer is truly the backbone of my active ministry. The more I have received in silence the more I will be able to give to those seeking my assistance.

Being more honest with my own weaknesses and limitations has helped me greatly to be more aware of others' needs. I know now more than ever before that I walk the same path with my brothers and sisters. Compassion is a quiet, reassuring power.

When the phones are ringing, and people are waiting outside my door to see me, and the bookkeeper is concerned about bills to be paid, and I'm curious about why the Servant General wants me to call him back ... I begin to wonder what my priestly calling is all about.

I often feel it would be much easier and more in the Spirit of Jesus to pour coffee, serve food and exchange meaningful conversation with the poor and rejected. Living the mission and message of Jesus, so simply revealed in the Gospels, for some reason or another can become so complex. Very often the desired end — to reveal the spirit of Jesus — can become smothered in just keeping the ship afloat. These are frustrating moments in my life and in the life of any Christian who truly desires to have Christ living within.

When these perplexing thoughts come upon me, I yearn for quiet times so that I might once again bring into focus my Christian endeavors. Moments spent in silent prayer are precious.

These moments can be captured in the midst of a busy day, early in the morning, or at the end of the day if I so will. I am convinced that solitude is a state of mind.

If I had the opportunity of hiding away for a few days, taking a long walk in the stillness of the woods, or going off to a desert place, I would grasp the opportunity, but for me this would be a luxury. I am forced to create quiet times in the midst of ever increasing demands on my time and energy.

In silent prayer I open my heart to listen to God. Things begin to fall into place when I am able to transcend the demands of the moment. Then I am able to return to daily happenings, renewed in my commitment to be a servant.

When I find myself role-playing, when my calling is not uppermost in my thoughts and actions, these prayerful moments of encounter are the only way for me to remain honest with my God, myself and the people for whom I am responsible.

Time is too precious to let myself be fooled or caught up in delusions. Moments of silence enable me to assess the measure of my service. I become keenly aware of those occasions when I have neglected my commission to love in the Spirit of Jesus. There are times when I miss the opportunity to give a word of encouragement, to express my genuine concern, to extend my hand in friendship, or just to be present when needed. I profess to believe, but so often my actions fail to reveal a profound faith that would urge me on to greater sharing and giving.

I come away from these moments of confrontation with this practical conclusion: that things are not always the way I would like them to be, that I myself am not so good or so kind or so hard-working as I would like to believe. And yet —*and yet*—with each sunrise there is a new day, a new challenge, a new opportunity for doing better. A new tomorrow is ever my Christian hope.

7

A Time to Grow

One snowy winter morning in 1956, when I was a student at St. Joseph's Seminary in Teutopolis, Illinois, I awoke with a strong feeling of inner peace. It was going to be a good day in the Lord.

As I threw on my heavy woolen habit in preparation for praying the Divine Office, followed by Mass, I experienced a sense of excitement within. For some time I had been undergoing much confusion and frustration in my desire to seek my Lord with my whole soul, my whole mind, and my whole heart. I was longing for a simple plan of action to which I could hold fast in my spiritual journey.

One event on that day so many years ago brought an answer to my prayers. The first book I picked up as I prepared for class was *The Faith Explained* by the late Father Leo Trese. In chapter one he posed three simple questions, the answers to which I feel are at the very core of Christian commitment. These questions may seem simplistic but working out the answers is nothing less than profound. In every retreat I give, these three questions are before me at all times. I will now state the questions. I will write a few words about each one and then leave the rest for your personal reflection.

Why am I here? I have been created in the image of my God for His honor and glory. I am precious in His sight. Even though I often stumble through life, I am unique in God's presence. He wills my salvation. He loves me. He forgives me. This, in faith, I am convinced of beyond any doubt. What I firmly believe of myself holds equally true for my neighbor. Each person who enters my life — in a brief encounter or a long, enduring relationship — is precious in the Lord. I must seek the vision of God in the saint and in the sinner. As I visit the local jail and meet the man who has just raped an innocent child, I am called to look through his brokenness to reaffirm my belief that he too is created to the image of his Maker. This vision of Jesus is hidden in

passion run wild, in pretense, in sham, but all this can be peeled away
in conversion of mind and heart. As a Christian it is my profound
privilege to communicate the love, the power of Jesus to this man. I
will speak to him as Christ would speak. I will remain close to Him in
prayer, knowing the power to heal is in my God.

Where am I going? My heart is restless until it rests in my God. I
firmly believe that union with my God in the life hereafter is but a
perfection of the love I strive for daily in my relationship with Him
now and the love I now express for my brothers and sisters. For the
Christian intent on going beyond measure in loving concern, this
present life is a foretaste of the life to come; the kingdom of heaven is
opened.

How am I going to get there? It is for me a daily struggled to put
on the mind and heart of Jesus. As I grow older I pray more fervently
for a deepening of my faith life. It is easy to settle for a comfortable
Christian existence. The enthusiasm needed to embrace new challenges in my quest for holiness can dry up so quickly. When this
happens, life is no longer lived abundantly. Stagnation sets in.

I frequently call to mind an infallible promise of Jesus: "Seek and
you shall find; knock and it shall be opened." If I pray with openness to
have revealed those obstacles that now hinder me in living out my
commitment to servanthood, my prayer will be answered. Whatever I
do for myself will redound to the good of those I am called to serve.
With enlightenment of mind will also come the strength of purpose
needed to make the necessary changes in my life that will enable me to
become a more fit instrument in His service. I will live life abundantly
and die graciously in the Lord.

You are, and I am, called to greatness. This is my allotted time. I
cannot hestitate. I too must surrender. Then only can God do great
things in you and in me.

Why am I here? Where am I going? How am I going to get there?
These three questions have profound ramifications for myself and
those I am called to serve in His name.

Lord, my heart is restless. Whatever the cost, I desire a fuller conversion of mind and heart. Let my sins be forgiven, haunting memories forgotten, broken relationships healed, compulsive patterns of action thwarted, unfounded fear resolved, distorted thinking made right. I am called to greatness of spirit. Keep me always aware of how precious I am. I now see you as in a mirror, but someday I will see you face to face. Give me the burning desire to spend myself and be spent in your service.

O Lord, realizing I cannot give what I do not have, grant me the singleness of purpose to seek a vibrant interior life enabling me to grow in your love and the love of my neighbor.

I am so often asked by those who are serious about their quest for the inner life, What signs indicate progress in living out the mission of Jesus? If I am truly making every effort to seek first the kingdom of God for myself and those I am called to serve, I will mirror the quest in my attitude of mind and heart. Life in the Spirit of Jesus is manifested in our every thought, word and deed.

Peace of mind and heart is precious to the Christian, who rejoices in the good and stands firm in faith when the waters of daily life become rough. Peace of mind and heart is the reward for the one who strives daily to put on the Lord Jesus Christ. Faith will be so strong that no matter how difficult life becomes there will be the underlying strength of purpose to see all things working for good. If my life has real meaning, if I am seeking to put Jesus first in my life, peace of mind and heart will follow as day follows night.

In a mature spiritual person there is always a zest for life. I will not settle on a comfortable plateau of self-righteousness but rather see each day as an opportunity to grow in a closer union with Jesus and my brothers and sisters. I have met people of eighty or ninety years of age who were very young. The joy of Christian living is found in those who look upon each waking moment as a precious occasion to live in the Spirit of Jesus among those they love, those they are called to serve. Whatever I do to the least of my brothers or sisters is done unto Jesus. This zest for life can be achieved from the hospital bed, from times spent in prayer, from the community table, from the assembly line, from the checkout counter, from the ordinary meetings and events of everyday life.

My willingness to reach out to all is a true measure of my spiritual maturity. Love for my neighbor must never dim. It is vitally important that at all times I view each individual, the one easily loved and the one who turns me off, as created to the image and likeness of God, as a temple of the Spirit, as little less than an angel. This is no simple task.

I have reached some degree of spiritual maturity when I accept responsibility for my own mistakes, my own sins. I am much aware of my humanness, the times I am selfish, the times I am selfless. When I sin I am willing to admit my temporary defeat, beg God's forgiveness and again be about my Father's business. There is no time for self-pity or, even worse, blaming my setbacks on others.

Spiritual maturity is evident when my concern for others does not depend so much on how they my react to me. Like any other human being, I need words of encouragement, a sense of gratitude. However, in spending myself and being spent for the good of those entrusted to my care, my faith in the preciousness of the person standing before me must deepen with every encounter. Any other approach will meet with stinging disappointment and ultimate frustration. On the other hand, in faith I am deeply convinced that in giving I too will receive.

To be spiritually mature I must possess the ability in this day to face openly the doubts and uncertainties that crowd into my life and the lives of my people. It takes a truly humble man to admit he does not have all the answers and yet live and act in a spirit of genuine faith. I can speak eloquently about faith but frequently I find myself more concerned about certainty. I pray daily for a surrender in faith to become a living reality in my life: a faith so strong that I can feel, see and touch it in my life and the lives of those I serve.

Even after many years of priestly service, doubts often crowd into my mind. I do not falter in my belief in God or in His Son. My doubts seem to center more around my own efficacy as a priest, my own spiritual worth.

My prayers can appear to be hollow, empty words that echo off the walls and rise no higher than the ceiling of my room. I even wonder at times about the good I strive to do for others in His name. So much goes unnoticed by the world and has meaning only in the other world of the spirit, a world I cannot feel, see or measure.

Is it possible to grind out spiritual victories in this world where disagreements, indifference, selfishness, vested interests and broken relationshps can be witnessed daily, felt deeply and touched at the very core of my being?

When these depressing thoughts come before me I think of those seventy-two disciples that Christ sent before Him into the towns and villages He planned to visit. He warned them sternly that they might be mocked and persecuted. We are like lambs among wolves.

These disciples undoubtedly went about their mission walking over hot sand, steep hills, preaching to mixed crowds, knocking at doors, asking to see the sick, giving comfort to the sinners and announcing the coming of the Lord. These efforts took place in the visible world, but in faith they achieved tremendous spiritual gains. On their return, Jesus told them He had seen Satan fall like lightning from heaven. Spiritual victories of lasting value had been won through the persevering effort of His disciples.

I am spiritually mature when I am willing to make changes in my lifestyle that are necessary to my good and the good of those I serve. In other words, I am committed as a Christian — even more so as a priest — to growth.

Spiritual maturity demands a high degree of tolerance for the behavior of others. I can readily accept the sinner without stern judgment or condemnation. I seek forgiveness and enlightenment for the sinner as I desire it for myself. I strive to be conscious of where my people are coming from, all the circumstances surrounding their everyday existence, the pressures brought upon them, their efforts just to survive in this world of ours. I beg for the grace to be an instrument of enlightenment and peace in their lives.

Maturity is shown in a willingness to live in the present. I can waste so much time worrying over the past, over the things I did twenty years ago, by regretting and regressing, by wishing I could do it over or undo it all. The past is the past. The future is not mine to know. I live in the present. Jesus must be found in today's events. The now is mine to put on the mind and heart of my Master. The people I meet this day are *all* important. They may very well be the last I will meet or serve. Today may they see a reflection of Jesus in me.

Along with singleness of purpose there is a need to seek balance in my life. I need a time for prayer wherein I deepen my own convictions. I cannot give what I do not have. There is also a time to go into action. My prayer life is only real when it reveals itself in my sensitivity to my brothers and sisters. I can go off into a deserted place and pray my heart out, but if my prayer life fails to make me aware of the needs of others, I can smother myself with selfishness. It is in the everyday happenings of life, where I rub shoulders with my brothers and sisters, that the strength of my inner life will be tested. Proper balance is important when striving to walk in the Master's footsteps. There is Mount Tabor, the ecstasy, but along with the ecstasy is the daily cross, the agony.

A spiritually mature person will not run too far without looking into himself in silent prayer, where truth will be revealed. Delusion can easily work into my life if I fail to look inward and beg for the grace to do all for the right reasons.

A mature Christian accepts himself or herself as a unique creation of a loving God. In my uniqueness can be found the raw materials to be fashioned into the likeness of my Lord. The mind of my Lord will be formed and tested in my own uniqueness. I will not be another Cure' of Ars, a Little Flower, another Francis of Assisi. I am called to holiness as Claude Buchanan. Conceived in a rapture of love in the spring of 1928 and born in February of 1929 with the potential to be a sharing, giving, loving person. I am accepted in both my weaknesses and in my strengths with my limitations and my God-given capabilities. His power can flow in me. The energy, the perseverance, and the courage needed to unlock the potential within me are released to love as my Lord loves me and all those created in His image. All this will come about only when I acknowledge and believe in my own uniqueness.

A mature Christian is keenly aware that salvation is linked to his brothers and sisters. "By this will all men know you are my disciples: that you love one another as I love you." On the day of judgment I will not be asked how many Masses I have offered, how often I have fasted, the time spent in prayer, or money given. All these outward manifestations of belief have but one purpose: to bring me into a closer relationship with my God and to move me to love my neighbor as I am called to love myself. If religious observances fail to stir up within me a greater love for my God and my neighbor, then all this effort is in vain. My Lord freely gave His life for me. "No greater love has a man than to give his life for his friend." Sacrifice is the measure of my love for my God and for my neighbor.

A mature Christian constantly testifies to the power of prayer. Prayer is an honest communication with my Lord. My intimate relationship with my Lord will depend on the full and frank sharing of my innermost thoughts and feelings. Honest prayer has the power to move mountains in bringing about a true transformation of soul. Slowly but surely my Lord becomes the one center, the one reason, the one motivating force, the one direction and purpose of my every living moment.

A mature Christian is a servant not only in word, but in daily living. Pope, bishop, priest, minister, and all God's children find their indentity as Christians in direct proportion to their willingness to serve. President Jimmy Carter asked the Holy Father, who was visiting the White House, how he withstood the constant adulation of those surrounding him and of the crowds in the street. Pope John Paul II replied that it was his most difficult task to be ever conscious that he too was but a servant of God. Power and authority can corrupt the best intentions.

My willingness to serve extends not only to those in my immediate Christian community but to those far less appealing — the indifferent, the rejected of society, the homeless, the AIDS victims, the mentally ill — those who just do not fit into my pattern of daily living. It is not difficult for me to feel sorry for such people, to remember them in my prayers, to send money to relieve their sufferings, but it is another thing to associate with them, to share intimately in their pain, their hurt. How often I have passed someone with a flat tire; I feel for them but can always find an excuse for not stopping to give an assist. I think of my Lord washing the feet of His apostles. I need more pails of water, more towels in my life if I am truly to be a servant. I must learn to serve the small and the great of life. This requires a spirit of healing, of reconciliation. Jesus approached everyone He met with compassion and more. He took on our human condition, bore our offenses, suffered our pain and defeat. In the spirit of compassion the healing strength of forgiveness reaches out to enfold the weak, the fallen, the defeated, in a Christ-like embrace.

Another quality of spiritual maturity is joy. A profound sense of peace and joy permeates a person who seeks harmony with all he or she encounters. How often dissatisfaction, bitterness, a sense of futility and frustration buffet us when we are contending with others because of our selfish designs of pampered pride. The greatest sorrow I personally experience is to see people so caught up in self that their ability to love, their peace and joy are totally frustrated. A peaceful, joyful Christian quells agitation, smothers strife, quiets angry outbursts, soothes troubled hearts, lives with a sense of well-being and unity with all creation. This peace, this inner joy, is the experience of every Christian living life abundantly in the Spirit of Jesus.

I must readily admit I do not have it all together. Some press steadily along. It is my lot to get up for a while only to stumble. The presence of my Lord is revealed in my willingness to continue to get up and seek another new beginning. I do at times dream of when the comfortable state will arrive in which I will have it all together, when struggling, striving and new beginnings become past history. I will get there. You will get there. Our Lord does not expect us to have it all together. No one arrives here on earth. When you and I see our Lord face to face in the kingdom, His image will be revealed fully in us. Until then we will follow in His steps, living in His love.

Life in the spirit is full and meaningful, a possession no one can take from me. But I must have the courage to claim it, to live for my Lord in the small and great of my daily life.

I will in this spirit touch my brothers and sisters not so much with my words or my writings, but by the example of my life, my commitment to servanthood. My Lord is alive this day in me. My living Lord is revealed through me in my compassion for those suffering in body and soul. I will make every effort to help free them from crippling worries, anxieties, feelings of inferiority, hates and guilts, so they can acknowledge their greatness: my Lord can then do great things in them.

I pray to let the Lord be present in all the circumstances of my life. My Lord is not just another add-on to an already hectic life. To seek my Lord first is not a matter of preferred order but an all-embracing reality penetrating every aspect of my daily life. All things must be grounded in Him: my busy schedule; the unforeseen events of each day; the successes, the failures of my daily struggles; the unexpected visitor; the sudden call to reach out in loving concern; my willing acceptance of all my brothers and sisters — the faith-filled, the doubting, the indifferent, the unbelievers. In my daily quest to put on the mind and heart of my Lord I am seeking a genuine transformation.

Imagine a two-foot-long steel bar one inch thick. In this form it is worth around $10.00. If this same piece of steel is molded into two pairs of horseshoes of good quality it can be revalued at $26.00. This same piece of steel recast into a piece of machinery takes on the value of $3,286. In the form of fine steel springs for watches its value increases to $250,000.

The same pattern of upgrading applies well to the Christian who is willing to pay the price of discipleship. We can settle for mediocrity or we can freely choose to rise to greatness of spirit. My Lord can move mountains but He does not move me unless I am willing to let Him move within me. The Lord works in us in varied ways.

You and I have dared to dream of becoming saints. When we return to the stark reality of the everyday world, we soon stumble over the contradictions so evident in our lives. We are appalled by the selfishness that works away at our best resolves. We are humiliated by the lack of consistency found in our human condition. We want to bring about changes within ourselves, but the path to perfection is not an easy one to walk.

Without any doubt the most difficult task in my quest for spiritual maturity is to bring about necessary changes in myself so I may more effectively reveal Jesus to others. Change can be as painful as the suffering of the mother who bore me. But I can never forget that I have been chosen from among men to bear witness to the love Jesus has for all His people. Nothing else matters. I am called to holiness. I have been branded with the name of Jesus.

My desire to grow daily in union with Jesus requires that I bring about changes in my life. Making this painful effort will prove the sincerity of my desires. It is easy for me to reach an acceptable level in my faith life and be content to remain there. The trouble is I lose ground. My sense of the Christian challenge and what it demands of me grows faint. This is a sad condition, for I know, in faith, that God can do great things in me.

Knock and it shall be opened. Seek and you shall find. Are we willing to take up the cross and follow in His footsteps? In prayer I beg for the crooked paths in my life to be made straight. I want to be conscious of the times I am selfish, when I fail to go beyond convenience in service to my brothers and sisters, when I fail to love as He has loved me. I want to be aware of the time wasted, never to pass my way again. I want to know when I am puffed up with my own self-importance. When I lack sensitivity to the hurt, rejection, defeat and sinfulness of my brothers and sisters, I ask that my failures stand out like a sore thumb.

Insights gained in prayer can be forgotten when I return to the give-and-take of everyday living. Writing out my good intentions will make me aware here and now of the opportunities that will cross my path this day to think, to speak, to act in the Spirit of Jesus. Taking the time to jot down my priorities for this day will be an evident sign of my resolve to put the kingdom of God first in my life and in the lives of those I serve. A simple method, but one that assures consistent growth in loving concern. Pope John XXIII used this method very effectively in his *Journey of a Soul.*

I value the gift of friendship. A committed friend is one I know will be honest with me. He is ready with words of encouragement. He confronts me with the truth even when it hurts. He helps me in my struggle to change, to put on the new man. He urges me on to holiness, to always seek the best. As Scripture says, "A man helped by his brother is like a strong city."

If I am ever willing to be ready to make those necessary changes in my ongoing quest for spiritual maturity, then I will truly live life abundantly in the Lord. The rejected will experience the warmth of my love, the indifferent will see the kingdom of God in me, the sick will be strengthened by the depth of my faith, the lonely will be urged on to give themselves in prayer and service to others, the defeated will look forward to a new day, those who have much will be convinced that it is in giving that they too will receive.

Lord, grant me the grace to see myself for what I am so I may become what I ought to be. This I ask in your name.

Steps to Maturity

Maturity is the ability to handle frustration, control anger, and settle differences without violence or destruction.

Maturity is patience. It is the willingness to postpone gratification, to pass up the immediate pleasure or profit in favor of the long-term gain.

Maturity is perseverance, sweating out a project or a situation in spite of opposition and discouraging setbacks.

Maturity is unselfishness, responding to the needs of others.

Maturity is the capacity to face unpleasantness and disappointment without becoming bitter.

Maturity is the gift of remaining calm in the face of chaos. This means peace, not only for ourselves, but for those with whom we live and for those whose lives touch ours.

Maturity is the ability to disagree without being disagreeable.

Maturity is humility. A mature person is able to say, "I was wrong." He is also able to say, "I am sorry." And when he is proven right, he does not have to say, "I told you so."

Maturity is the ability to make a decision, to act on that decision, and to accept full responsibility for the outcome.

Maturity means dependability, integrity, keeping one's word. The immature have excuses for everything. They are the chronically tardy, the no-shows, the gutless wonders who fold in the crises. Their lives are a maze of broken promises, unfinished business, and former friends.

Maturity is the ability to live in peace with that which we cannot change.

8

A Time to Give

Travel with me in your imagination as I describe a rather typical summer experience in rural Missouri. Picture a car that has pretty well seen its day rumbling down a gravel road. The temperature is ninety-five degrees in the shade. The windows of the car are down. The visible dust of the road rolls in upon the occupants. The car turns into our driveway. Two gentlemen step out of the car a bit dusty and bedraggled with a few books tucked under their arms and pamphlets in their hands. With great courtesy they introduce themselves as Jehovah's Witnesses. I respond in a friendly way, informing them that I am Catholic and a priest. The conversation usually does not last too long but our parting is friendly. They climb back into the car and in a cloud of dust make their way to our neighbor's gate.

This experience always causes me to sit back for a few moments in quiet questioning. I surely do not dwell on their religious beliefs but cannot help but admire their persevering zeal that seems to be the fruit of much personal inconvenience. I firmly believe my Church has the full deposit of truth. I treasure the inner life of my Church that has brought forth in every age so many holy men and women and charity beyond comprehension. I hold so precious the sacramental life of my Church, especially my fervent belief in Jesus' real presence in the Eucharist. But after the visit from the Jehovah's Witnesses I wonder just how much I am willing to give of myself in bringing what I hold so dear to my brethren on the other side of the fence. I fear I am content so often to settle for a Church that is rather than a Church that could be. In all honesty, would I be willing to spend my time going from door to door in very unfavorable conditions to share my beliefs with those who have not had the opportunity to experience the inner joy of my own convictions?

Would I travel the dusty gravel road? Could I inspire my people to travel with me?

Again, in your imagination, travel with me to the home of a Mormon family in Salt Lake City. They are spending the evening with their eighteen-year-old son who will leave the next morning with 120 other young people on a chartered jet for the Mormon Missions of South Africa. He is willing to give two years of service witnessing to his Mormon beliefs. Could that be the price of discipleship that Christ demanded of his first followers? Again I find myself asking the nagging question: how many teenagers among my people would be willing to leave home and friends as an expression of their own appreciation for the faith that is theirs?

I speak of the numbers of families I have in my parish. Do the numbers remain pretty well the same year in and year out? Or, do I find that the example of my life and the vibrant faith of my people attract others in good numbers to the richness of our belief? Sometimes I fear that I and my people settle for the captive audience that is ours by birth rather than a Church filled with zeal to gather into the fold those who have not experienced the Good News. As Pope John XXIII once said, "Goodness attracts goodness."

It boils down to my willingness to pay the full price of discipleship and all that it involves. Only then will the spark of my zeal urge my people on to greater things. Who knows — they may travel the dusty road with me.

I have chosen to bring the *saving* message of Jesus to all who enter my daily life. I do this not only by my words but by my example. How clearly do I mirror Jesus in my words, in my thoughts, in my actions? Any conflicting interest that detracts from my calling must go! Otherwise I will waste precious time and run the risk of living in delusion. I enjoy laughter. I appreciate the tears of someone hurting. I rejoice in the success of another. I am compassionate when a dream fails to come true. I treasure the moments spent with a friend. I understand the pain of loneliness. As the years pass I fervently hope to become more and more all things to those I have been called to serve.

At all costs I must avoid a comfortable priesthood wherein I find myself going through the hoop of priestly existence, void of spirit and life. Such a daily existence will only produce boredom and a lack of

real purpose in my life. My happiness, my peace of mind, my fulfillment will be found in the core of my calling as a priest. It will be
discovered in the joy of a grateful penitent; the solace found in sharing
the grief of someone who has lost a loved one, a friend; the placing of
His real presence into the hands of a communicant; the preaching of a
sermon breathing spirit and life, urging my people to become more
sharing, more loving, more giving at home, at play, at work. It is in
giving that I too will receive. This is truly what my calling as a priest is
all about.

Jesus was a compassionate man, ever sensitive to the everyday
needs of His people, but even more to their innner conflicts of the
spirit. To be compassionate in imitation of my master is no easy task.
It takes daily persevering effort to put on the mind of Christ. I find
myself wondering at times just how much I want to become involved
in the problems of others. Am I for the long haul? Am I compassionate
in the true sense of the word?

I remember many years ago asking an older priest who had truly
spent himself in the service of his Master and his people what qualities
he thought were needed to be compassionate. Knowing the priest well,
I wanted to know what made him so responsive to the needs of his
people over so long a time without becoming weary in the battle.

The good father thought for a few moments and then spoke of
three qualities he believed necessary.

The first quality he mentioned was empathy, the ability to feel
with another person. I can at times become so wrapped up in my own
little world that it becomes near to impossible to appreciate where
another person is coming from. Empathy demands that I empty
myself so I am freed up to project my own self into the consciousness
of another who is hurting in body and soul. This hurt is not always
perceivable to the naked eye. It takes a sixth sense that is the priceless
gift of the compassionate person. At times I find it a real struggle to
have understanding charity for all. Some people I want nothing to do
with. When this happens I reflect on Francis of Assisi's conversion.
Francis had a great repugnance for the lepers of his time. He would
travel long distances to avoid them. His conversion came when he

finally had the courage to kiss the hands of a leper. Only then did God do great things in Francis.

The second quality the priest mentioned was fortitude, the persevering spirit needed to care for a person over a long period of time. Sometimes I fear to become involved, knowing all the demands that will be made on me. It is not difficult to make that first visit to the hospital, spend a few moments with a troubled person, give a few dollars to a family in need and then steer away from further involvement. It surely does take courage for me to travel the long road with someone who needs my continuing support. However, when I have the courage, the willingness to go all the way in the spirit of my Master, I begin to taste the sweetness of the Lord.

The habit of giving was the third quality the older priest mentioned as necessary to be a compassionate person. For me the habit of giving is hard to come by. This day as every day I must ask myself where can I give. If I do not plan at morning prayer how I can best serve my people this day, much goes undone and precious time is wasted. I find it most helpful to jot down in the morning those people I wish to visit, someone who deserves a word of thanks, encouragement or confirmation, a letter to be written, people who have asked for a remembrance in my prayers. In this way I hope to develop a habit of giving. I also hope to live my life more abundantly.

Empathy, courage, the habit of giving — perhaps the older priest hit the nail right on the head. And perhaps there are still other qualities hidden in the tenderness of the compassionate heart.

I pray daily for the wisdom of knowing the moment: the moment to act or not to act, the moment to speak, the moment to be silent.

To achieve the grace of knowing the right moment I must constantly reach out to those I am called to serve, ever sensitive to their needs at the present moment. It may be a time to laugh, a time to weep. It may the the moment when my silent presence is all that is called for. It may be the moment when words of encouragement are desperately needed. It may be the moment that demands tough love — I must say it as it is even though it hurts. It may be the moment when I reveal my own fears and doubts so the one seeking my help does not feel alone in his world of hurt and confusion. To know the moment demands the willingness to reach out beyond my own world and project myself into the consciousness of the one who is in some way asking for help.

Good timing, being aware of the moment, will often have me doing the unexpected: a word of encouragement to people who have given their time, their energy far beyond measure; the unexpected visit to the senior citizens' luncheon; the unexpected bouquet of flowers for the young mother dying of cancer; the unexpected visit to the family who lost their mother a few weeks ago and now is left alone with their grief; the unexpected day off for the housekeeper who has given so many years of dedicated service; the unexpected financial assistance to a family in real need who find it so difficult to ask for help; the unexpected visit to a brother priest who is experiencing difficulty in his new assignment; the unexpected letter to someone burdened with hurt; the unexpected note of thanks to someone who has been most thoughtful; or just chatting with an old-timer who finds great joy in reminiscing about days gone by. The unexpected expression of love carries with it a powerful message, a message that can often bring great comfort to the receiver.

Being keenly aware of the moment helps me anticipate the needs of others. The future is not a closed book. In loving concern I can offer my assistance before I am asked. This often lifts a burden from someone who finds it most difficult to seek help even when in real need.

Knowing the moment demands great patience. I am forced to make a pact with myself not to act too quickly in times of anger or personal frustration. Just when I am about to say I can give no more this day, the phone will ring or someone will appear at the door, in need of a compassionate heart. I then thank God for being present, for my being conscious of the moment. It keeps me aware of how timing can be decisive.

Pope John XXIII made a wise statement in his diary *The Journal of a Soul*: "See everything, overlook a lot and improve a little." At first glance the statement does not look very idealistic. However, for the committed Christian striving daily to walk in the footsteps of the Lord, this statement is encouraging and most real. On my life's journey I climb many mountains and walk through long valleys in my constant search for a closer union with my Lord.

It is my fervent desire to look upon each day as a new beginning. I can do very little about the past. I cannot boast of the future. The precious moment now before me is mine to be lived abundantly in the presence of my Lord and in loving service to my brothers and sisters. This is my allotted time. The gift of life is priceless and every moment is to be treasured.

Starting this day, I will double my effort to capture time to be with my Lord in quiet prayer. My prayer will be simple. "Ask, and it will be given to you." When I open my heart, words flow very simply, very naturally. I want to speak to Him as my friend, one who knows intimately my strengths, my weaknesses, my desire for holiness and my daily struggle with the tendencies within that often war against my desire for intimacy with God. I can hide nothing from my Lord. My Lord knows of my struggles and walks at my side in good times and in bad times.

I also want to bring before my Lord all those who have asked for my prayers. It is a privilege to pray for my brothers and sisters. I am convinced of the power, the saving grace, of prayer to affect our lives.

Starting this day, I will make greater effort to communicate to you your unique preciousness in the Lord we both adore. There will never be another you or another me. We are both called to an intimate union with Him. When we live more fully in His presence He will do great things in us. To truly be servants in imitation of our Lord will force us to put aside personal prejudice, our own often preconceived ways of thinking and acting, our feeling of self-importance, our desire for security. We will be urged in the Spirit to pick up the towel and pail of water and wash the feet of our neighbors.

Starting this day, I will remind myself to really listen to you in times of joy, in times of sorrow, in times of success, in times of failure or when you need someone just to be present. At this very moment in time you are the most important person in my life. In you I see the image of my Lord. How would my Lord speak at this moment? How would He respond in compassion at this moment? I pray that when in your presence I appreciate the sanctity of the given moment when two pilgrims walk side by side.

Starting this day, I will reach out gently to touch my brothers and sisters with words of affirmation and genuine concern. I will reach out in friendship, walking not in front of my friend, not in back of my friend, but truly at his or her side. I want to console you in your inner hurt and disappointment. I want to rejoice in your times of inner joy and expectation. I want to live life abundantly with you at my side. I want to look forward with you to the day we see our Lord face to face.

My problems and your problems are not to be solved all at once. We gradually become transformed into the likeness of our Lord. I will be constantly mindful of my humanness, my brokenness. I will be ever patient with myself and with you. I will not demand perfection of you until I am perfect. You are safe!

9

A Time to Die

After Sunday Mass I took a stroll through a small cemetery deep in the heart of the Ozarks. I have made so many visits to the cemetery that the moss-covered headstones and the people buried beneath them have become like well-known friends to me. This particular Sunday I found myself passing by a stone whose epitaph was almost indistinguishable. The many years, some 116, had played a hard game with the headstone.

I got on my knees to brush away the crust formed by many hot summers and bitterly cold winters. The stone marked the resting place of someone's beloved wife. Beneath the name was not a biblical quotation but, for all purposes, a statement of fact. It read, "To my beloved wife: ever she sought the best, ever found it."

When beginning my afternoon stroll I found myself in a rather depressed mood. Concerns seemed to be crowding in on me and I had no ready solutions. No single, overwhelming problem—just a combination of things.

I was daily witnessing a close priest friend of mine dying of cancer. He had given many dedicated years to the priesthood but, as the end came near, he was so much alone. His brother priests and the people he had served so faithfully seemed rather indifferent to the pain and loneliness he now so patiently endured.

A young couple I had worked with for many years had made their decision to seek a divorce. My thoughts actually were more with the children involved and their feelings of bewilderment. It is so easy to write off or never really consider the hurt experienced by children when their parents separate. They vividly remember those happy moments when the family was one in spirit. Now it had come to an abrupt end.

I also was thinking of an elderly lady who had just recently lost her husband. She told me the evening hours were the worst. Her ten children were married and scattered throughout the country. This left her alone with thoughts of yesterdays, the Midnight Masses attended by the family, the many First Communions, weddings, Thanksgivings, all the comings and goings of a large family. Now she was alone with memories of the past.

My own failure to be more sensitive to those I serve in His name was also bothering me. I seem to waver so much in my resolves. This is my allotted time. I want to use it wisely. I want to love as Jesus loved.

As I looked at the faded engraving, those eight words — "ever she sought the best, ever found it" — began to haunt me. A century ago this woman had lived through a war in which brother fought brother, friends were forced to kill one another. She may have even lost a boy in battle. She too must have experienced depression, even despair at times. Things did not always work out for her, but the inscription on the headstone must have come from the heart of someone who knew her well. The epitaph was a profound compliment. I felt courage in the words, a certain sense of dignity, of triumph.

Sometimes I let my problems and the problems of my people become all-absorbing. They in some odd way become the center of life, not mere guests at my table. I surely want to be ever sensitive to my real needs and the needs of my people. However, I cannot afford to let the dark side of life obscure all the good that can be accomplished in the midst of the pain and anguish. I am called to comfort my priest friend who is dying. I am called to bring meaning and purpose into the shattered lives of my people even though at times they refuse to yield in a spirit of faith. The lonely of heart must be convinced that God can still do great things in them. I need not spend my time meditating on hurt feelings, misguided goals and seemingly hopeless situations. It is my calling as a man of God to bring the peace of Jesus into every facet of living and of dying.

The wife whose grave I stood by did not let life conquer her. If the barely visible engraving was a true expression of her spirit, she conquered life and found the best. It is for me to search out the good in all men and women and strive to bring peace from the bitter lessons of life, to reveal again and again the wonder of living in the Spirit of Jesus.

As a priest I must often tell those who come to me for assistance not to let their defeats defeat them. The pain of sorrow over the death of someone very close; the disappointment experienced when plans, so well prepared, crumble; the anguish felt by parents when their children reject sacred values; the lack of gratitude from those who have been given so much — at times we all experience the bitter taste of defeat, wondering if we can face another day.

For some twelve years, as procurator for our community, Servants of the Paraclete, I have had the daily privilege to share intimately in the lives of many of our benefactors—priests, sisters, brothers, laity. Each mail brings letters revealing the tragic defeats so many are called to endure in a spirit of faith. Some of their stories are almost beyond comprehension. I often wonder how my faith would measure up in like circumstances.

Here are but a few of the stories crying out for an understanding ear and a willingness on my part to carry in some vicarious way some of their burden in thought and in prayer. These pleas for help have convinced me of the strength of the human spirit, the miracles of grace worked in the lives of ordinary people.

I think of the elderly nun who had given some forty-seven years of dedicated service to the Church; she now has been asked by her small community to return to her relatives since the community can no longer afford to care for her in her declining years. In some way I experience her feelings of rejection after so much time and energy willingly given. Now she is out in the cold. In the past there was always an abundance of younger sisters sending in their monthly salaries for the support of those who served before them.

My thoughts travel to the home of a young teenager recently shot by accident; the bullet traveled through his spine and pierced his aorta. An artificial aorta is now supplying blood to the boy's lower regions. He is also paralyzed from his lower back to his feet. The doctors now wonder if his body will eventually reject the plastic aorta. His parents, ordinary people, treasure every moment of life their boy is given, but they are also obliged to pay $65,000 plus the cost of ongoing care.

Then comes to mind a priest who is struggling daily with his vocation. He is hanging by a thin thread. He feels that the spirit of his calling is gone. He no longer finds any inner joy in the priesthood that has been his for fifteen years. Father is asking himself if he made a serious mistake in being ordained. Is there peace of mind, a greater sense of fulfillment to be found on the other side of the fence? He is torn between the commitment he made and what might be.

A devoted wife comes to mind who is requesting prayers that her husband find a job. They are already three payments behind on their house and their children are in need of much dental care. All their dreams have come tumbling down because a car plant has been forced to close its doors.

What profound faith and heroic courage is demanded of these ordinary people! Miracles of grace are often born in sudden tragedy.

In the early hours of a Friday morning the news came over the police scanner. Rod, the son of our local Presbyterian minister, was not at fault. He met head-on a pickup truck driven by a young man who was in the wrong lane with his lights off. Both Rod and the young man driving the pickup truck were killed instantly. I visited the funeral home the next day and had a long talk with Rod's father, a man steeped in faith and attuned to the spirit of his Master.

Both sets of parents arrived at the hospital in the early morning hours to find their sons pronounced dead. Max, our minister friend, was aware of the other mother's grief. Even though his son had been killed in an accident that had no real reason, an accident that should not have happened, he immediately went over to the mother to express his sorrow over the death of her son and to assure her that he and his wife felt no bitterness.

I am sure Rod's entire life passed through Max's mind as he and his wife drove to the hospital. The joy of his birth, the first steps he took, the nights he and his wife stood beside his bedside in time of illness, the many Christmases and Easters spent together as a family, his graduation, his hopes for the future. Yet Max, in a spirit of Christ-like forgiveness, was ready to extend his love and concern to the mother and family of the boy who had senselessly caused the death of his son.

This revealed to me in a very graphic way much about forgiveness. Max forgave without any reservations, without any recrimination. It is easy for us to forgive when our forgiveness is conferred as a favor. Or, even worse, we forgive but by word or deed hold a person's mistakes or sins over his head.

Our Lord, toward the end of His life, suffered the rejection of those so close to Him. He endured the fickleness of the people He so loved. He accepted the unjust accusations of the leaders of Israel. He suffered His passion and death on the cross and could still say, "Father, forgive them for they know not what they do." At the hospital, burdened with their own intense grief, Max and his wife expressed so well the spirit of life of our Lord. "Put on the mind of Christ."

After leaving the funeral home I could not help but think of how petty, how slow I have often been to forgive a supposed hurt, an unkind word, a considered rejection. I have sought and received forgiveness and yet how critical, how judgmental, how self-righteous I have been at times. I earnestly pray for the spirit of forgiveness exemplified by Max. It amounts to a profound faith in Jesus and His message. It is easy to play games with words and fail to live as Jesus did.

Religious belief can be shallow — the court of last resort. It can be used as a cheap salve but lacking any real depth. It can be blind and often impervious to the human hurt suffered by so many so very near at hand.

When a judge who has passed the death sentence desires to become a priest, he must seek a dispensation from the Holy See. When a former executioner desires to become a priest, he too must obtain a dispensation for ordination. Both the judge and the executioner, due to past experience, may have become less sensitive to the trauma of death. The dispensations are normally granted, but having to request them before ordination brings to mind the need for priests to be sensitive to the reality of death and the pain of loss experienced by loved ones.

I recently concelebrated a Mass where the celebrant asked his people if there were any urgent needs they would like the community of the faithful to remember during the sacrifice. I had come to worship with many things on my mind — nothing really earth-shaking, but just distracting enough to make me somewhat indifferent to the importance of what was now taking place in my presence.

The requests for assistance in prayer brought me completely around. The impact of those pleas for help shocked me into awareness. A couple present for Mass had just lost their baby after a struggle of two weeks on life supports. Their baby, conceived in love, was carried to full term with joyful longing. Now their prayer for understanding exposed the raw question, "Why?" We were asked to remember a father of five boys who was fast losing his battle with cancer. For a moment I tried to place myself in his mind and heart. How will his wife carry on with him no longer at her side? I thought of the tremendous stress placed on the entire family as they watched their dad fade away. What did the future hold for the individual members of his family who would soon be without the warmth of his daily presence, the security he represented, the words of encouragement he gave? The familiar hug, the strong handshake, would soon be but memories of times past. "Why?" We were asked to remember a couple who had decided to separate, go their own ways. At one time they had walked hand in hand. Their happy memories have now turned bitter. "Why?" The distractions I brought into the chapel were put aside. I found myself in the company of concerned people who were at this very moment sharing in the hurt of so many.

So often we are asked to pray for needs far distant: the starving in the areas of Africa devastated by drought, for peace among ancient enemies, for the moral strength of our office holders, for our spiritual leaders that they might truly be men and women of God. Sometimes I feel so inadequate to cope with these petitions. I surely believe in the efficacy of prayer. However, I find myself humbled before the magnitude of man's needs.

Sometimes I think the feeling of helplessness I experience before such general needs is God's way of reminding me to be ever aware of those brothers and sisters close at hand who are hurting, who need someone to reach out to them in loving concern. I want not only to pray for healings of the spirit; I desire to play a vital role in that healing process. I will seek out my brothers and sisters. I will affirm them in His love. I will walk with my brothers and sisters as we make our way to Him.

Let me, Lord, venture from the warmth of the womb — the security of my comfortable world — and enter a new birth, to live my calling more abundantly. Then the realities of life will not pass me by. I will walk the streets with the poor, the defeated. I will visit the rich and see their anguish and their slicing pain. Hurt is no respecter of persons. Self-love is carried by all. I will face this fact in myself and in those I serve. In myself, and in my people, I will seek a new tomorrow in your likeness.

The reality of life presses upon me. I cannot close my eyes to hurt, pain, the power of destructive forces, the unexplainable accident, the intentional cruelty. With renewed faith I place my hope in the awareness of God's providence.

There are three ascending levels of how one mourns: With tears — that is the lowest. With silent prayer — that is higher. And with resolve — that is the highest.

As I browsed through the greetings cards at our local drug store, I came across a selection of Father's Day cards. For the first time in many years I would not be selecting a Father's Day card. My father died in early May. A simple mishap brought his unexpected death. No fatal illness — just a small piece of meat lodged in his esophagus caused his death. In trying to remove the meat, his esophagus was pierced. A massive infection quickly set in and, after thirty days battling the infection, my father died.

My eighty-four-year-old mother was rushed to the hospital a few days before my father's death, suffering from sheer exhaustion. On the eve of my father's death I had the privilege of walking my mother to his bedside so she could hold his hand for the last time and bid him farewell after fifty-seven years of marriage.

My father and I did not experience a warm personal relationship. He found it most difficult to express his love. During his final days I realized how much I loved him. I would lean close to Dad's ear to tell him I loved him. I would kiss his forehead, treasuring the moment when he squeezed my hand in recognition. Due to life-support systems, my father was unable to speak. He tried to express himself —a pitiful sight — but could not utter a word. The doctors held out real hope that he would pull through so we had no choice but to leave the life supports on. I pray he now understands. The life supports would have been removed in minutes if hope had ceased.

At first I experienced great sadness. Even though we clashed many times, even though I wished he had expressed his love in ways I could have responded to, I would have my father back this day if I could play God. I miss his frequent visits to the farm, his fantastic sense of humor, his phone calls when he would speak without any introduction. I still have not opened the small plastic bag containing his clothes he wore the day he drove himself to the hospital. For a while it seemed to be all I had left of my father's earthly sojourn.

Every Christian must in some way work through the ascending levels of mourning after the death of someone close. There is a time for weeping, a time for silent prayerful reflection, and finally a time for firm resolve.

There is first the immediate sorrow of loss mingled with feelings of regret. I take so many things for granted among those I love dearly. There are the thoughtful calls that could have been made more often, the visits overlooked or too widely spaced, the real or, more often, imagined hurts I let grow out of proportion, the times I tried to change my father, forgetting he was his own man. In this first level of mourning I thought of what I could have done to make life a bit more pleasant for the one who in God's plan gave me life. These opportunities are now gone. There is a lesson to be learned.

In silent prayer balance began to enter my grieving process. There are many happy memories. I must never forget the many times my father and I rose above our human condition to greatness of spirit. We often sought a new tomorrow together, making every effort to forget the past. I treasure these happy memories. There is a lesson to be learned.

I live now. This is my allotted time to share myself with those I love so dearly. This is my time to love, to give of myself. The sad regret so often heard at the death of a loved one, "if only," can be changed to "the next time." The precious lesson to be learned from my father's recent death is for me to recognize those daily opportunities to reveal the love of Jesus to all who enter my life. From the time my feet hit the floor in the morning till I fall asleep in the late hours of night, I resolve to be ever sensitive to the needs of others. All the gold in the world cannot buy a moment of time once the date, month and time are written.

This is the time for me to make those concerned calls and visits, to write letters of hope, to offer words of encouragement, to extend my hand in forgiveness, to treasure those moments spent with a friend, to see the sanctity of every moment, to pray more fervently to be a servant to my brothers and sisters created in His image. I pray with Paul to begin with renewed fervor to spend myself and be spent in His service.

I have now moved from tears, to understanding in prayer, to resolve. There is no need for a Father's Day card this year. The strife is over for my father. His time to climb the mountain, to win the crown, is completed. This is my time to fight the good battle, to run the course, to win the victor's crown. Lord, let me be about my Father's business.

Two years after my father died, my mother made her Easter journey home. Mom had been in a semi-conscious state ever since suffering a severe stroke in early January. A few months later, on the night before she died, I went back to her room to place a kiss on her lips and tell her, "Mom, good night and go home, go home." These were to be my last words to my mother. A few hours later she too said good-bye to this world and went home.

It is difficult to pen these lines in her memory. Memories of my mother still flood my heart. When my brother closed the casket, Mom passed from my sight, never again to be seen in this life. At this moment I became totally aware that I would never again hold her hand, place a kiss on her lips or be able to tell my mother how much I loved her.

I firmly believe in life after death. It remains a mystery, but I cling to the words of Paul, "Eye has not seen, nor ear heard, nor has it entered into the minds of men what things God has prepared for those who love Him." Paul was given a vision of the third heaven and could not utter in human terms what he had witnessed. Faith, in the knowledge of our own resurrection, triumphs over the profound sorrow first experienced. I cannot understand the theory of our expanding universe. How then can I expect to comprehend seeing my Lord face to face? But, face to face, I will someday see my Lord, as I believe my dear mother now sees Him.

It would be easy to linger on memories of my mother. Often I could have been more sharing, more giving, more loving. At times I would let smallness blur the vision of my Lord in my mother. Sorrow and regret must give way to resolution. My mother fought the good battle. She climbed the mountain in her own unique way. Mom has won the crown for a life well lived. My mother's death urges me to use my given time in greater service to you, my brothers and sisters.

As a servant of the Paraclete I have often had the cherished opportunity to be at the bedside of a dying brother priest. These have been truly moments of grace for me. These moments have brought home the preciousness of the great gift given me: my priestly calling.

I can remember Father John singing, "Que sera, sera, whatever will be will be, the future's not ours to see, Que sera, sera," as he was being pushed down the corridor to the operating room for a life-or-death operation. Whatever God willed, John was ready to accept. John didn't make it. At the beginning of my homily for John's funeral Mass I sang his song. It said it all.

On Father Paul's last day, I was asked to read Scripture to him in his final hours. He demanded that I read Luke 18:10, the story of the righteous Pharisee and the tax collector. Paul's eyes lit up when I read loud and clear the words, "God, be merciful to me a sinner." After spending over fifty years as a priest in missionary territory, which undoubtedly made tremendous demands on his own spirit of giving and sharing, in his final hours he was asking God for mercy.

Father Phil spent his last day in a semi-coma, reciting over and over again the "Gloria" of the Mass. Father Phil had dropped out of the priesthood for many years, but on his return, he truly spent himself in the service of his people.

Sitting here in my library on an early fall day, I couldn't help but think back to the last visit I shared with a priest friend last summer. It had been a hot, humid day with not a breath of air stirring. The walk from my car to the door of Bob's retirement apartment brought sweat to my forehead. Bob offered me a cold drink the minute I entered his front room. His living quarters were very comfortable with the rays of the early morning sun flooding his sitting room. Without words being spoken we both were aware that this would be his last summer. There was precious little time to reminisce or dream of the future. My friend had but the present moment to hold dear.

After serving in the armed forces for ten years and landing with our men on the beaches of Normandy, Bob had been appointed pastor of a large parish. He had been known for his untiring zeal, for his sensitivity to the needs of his people. He was also most conscious of those priests serving at his side. He had a great ability to build community among his brother priests. He always sought the best in a brother priest and found it.

As I sat with Bob I experienced a sense of aloneness. For a man like Bob who had so generously served so many, I felt that his front room, kitchen, and bedroom should be filled with grateful people. But I am also fully aware that there are life conditions to be faced alone no matter how many friends we have, no matter how many people we have assisted in life's struggles. The approaching call of the Lord to come home is the last and most awesome human experience, to be willingly accepted in the Lord's time.

What do you say to a dying friend? I had come to encourage Bob but all words seemed to fail. Bob spoke. I listened.

"I am sure grateful for your visit. You came a long way in this beastly weather." I could not help but think of the long distances he had so frequently traveled to visit the sick. "When a person knows that his boat is pulling up on the other shore, he thanks God for the gift of friendship. I hope this is what heaven is all about. The hardest thing now is the pain. I don't know which is worse — the pain or the medication. I just pray not to be a burden to others. If need be I'll call the nine-eleven number." I was struck by this last statement. A man who had been so available to others, when in serious need of help, must in his last days call upon such impersonal help.

"I have taken so many things for granted. I've never been so grateful for my priesthood as in these last days. There have been the rough times, times when I botched things up, but the good Lord always won out. I just got up from the ground, dusted off my pants and began a new day. Praying comes a little hard now. My rosary is a lifesaver. I try to keep my mind on the words as I float through the mysteries. Sometimes I just sit in His presence. I pray to live each day to the fullest and to die graciously in His arms."

I intently listened to my friend. I felt enriched by the whole experience. Bob had lived his calling to the fullest. He did not fear death. Like Francis of Assisi, he awaited Sister Death confident the in mercy, goodness and love of his Lord. As he had so often raised his hands in forgiveness; he would now confidently receive final absolution. If we are to be judged by the love we have for one another, then Bob has it made hands down.

As I was leaving, Bob again thanked me for the visit. I had come to encourage him. I left his presence encouraged by his faith and spirit.

Then I realized I had listened rather than talked — probably the best thing I possibly could have done for a dying friend.

Father Bob now lives on in the minds he inspired, in the many projects he helped pioneer, in the lives he improved, in the hearts that loved him so dearly. His presence is ever with us.

As a priest lives, so he dies. Now, while I yet live, is my time to surrender to God's will, to die to myself. I can know all things, but if I fail to share my life in loving concern, I have become as Paul so aptly said, "a noisy gong, a clanging cymbal."

I sometimes find it increasingly difficult to give of my time and energy to those who are selfish, indifferent, lacking in gratitude or often just plain obnoxious. It is always easier to work with those who express a need for my ministry or to spend my time among the saved, those who are open to the Spirit of Jesus, making real effort to live out their Christian commitment. I do many good things but I am, especially as I grow older, more sorely tempted to spend my time in safe zones where I will not run into the troubled waters of indifference or downright rejection.

Knowing there is the danger of falling into a comfortable priesthood wherein I spend the vast majority of my time and energy among those who appreciate my ministry, I find it necessary each day to call to mind the fact that God wills the salvation of all men and women. Jesus would have suffered His entire passion and death on the cross for one person. This surely brings home in a dramatic way the preciousness of every person who enters my life, even those revealing little or no interest in the redeeming love of Jesus. My thoughts, my words, my hands must constantly reach out to touch all in His name.

Each week I visit our local county jail. A month or so ago a young man accused of murder threw his urinal at me in anger. You can imagine how cautiously I approached his private cell on my next visit. We are now on speaking terms. If not even a sparrow falls to the earth without our heavenly Father knowing it, then how precious this young man is in the eyes of God. I pray daily to build a bridge of understanding so he too can find strength and hope in the words Jesus spoke of Mary Magdalen: "Many sins have been forgiven her because she has loved much." Maybe over the long haul this one man will come to know himself and the mercy of his God. Then God can do great things in him even behind prison bars. In faith I know beyond a doubt that he is lovable.

A few weeks ago I met an elderly priest who had been through four alcoholic treatment programs, all to no avail. Father arrived a defeated man with a real chip on his shoulder. He was quick to pin his problem, the whys and wherefores of his drinking, on his bishop, on his fellow priests, on the people he served. Even though I have heard this story time and time again as a Servant of the Paraclete, I had to be careful not to turn father off in my heart. He must be given another chance so his lips will again reveal the love of God to many. It is often a real struggle with patience to work with a man who denies the obvious: his responsibility for taking the first drink. However, I am also keenly aware that many other priests have gone through numerous programs before the healing power of honesty with their God and their people won out. Again, Father will be most difficult to work with; but with persevering effort on the part of our dedicated staff there is a real hope for a new tomorrow. God alone knows the hurt, the pain, the defeat, the feeling of rejection he is now experiencing. He feels truly alone in the world. He needs a brother priest who will walk with him — not in front of him, not in back of him — but at his side.

A few years ago a boy arrived at the door of the home for teenage boys where I resided. J.R. had a fatal disease that afflicted every joint in his body. You could see the lesions on his arms and wrists. The medicine he was required to take each day to stay alive caused him to smell with a metallic odor that was most offensive. On the second day he was with us he threw his arms around me, imitating the affection so often expressed by the other boys who had been with us for a number of years. I received his embrace but was uncomfortable with it. The metallic smell got to me. When J.R. left my presence I actually sniffed my shirt. Then I realized how contrary this was to the Spirit of Jesus I so often speak about. Jesus would have come to this earth, suffered His passion and death on the cross just for J.R. Needless to say, J.R. became much loved by me.

I need only to glance at the cross in my room to know the love Jesus expressed for me. "No greater love has a man than he give his life for his friend." He urges me, He urges you, to love as He loves.

I pray to look upon each new day as an opportunity to grow in love with my God and with my brothers and sisters. This, I firmly believe, is the message of Jesus. It is easy to settle for much less; but I am only fooling myself by letting time, never to be given back, slip through my hands like sand through an hourglass. I desire to pass from this life not regretting what could have been.

10

Restoration, Healing and Wholeness

It is a quiet March evening at the Lake of the Ozarks. Behind my room is a cemetery that dates back over 150 years. In front of me is the lake now cold and sleeping. I rejoice in the memories of past summers. I look forward to the coming of spring, when the lake will again come alive, bringing pleasure to many. I also whisper a prayer for those laid to rest many years ago and now all but forgotten. They too experienced the joys and sorrows, successes and failures of life. I pray they fought the good battle and now see their God face to face. This small cemetery makes me ever conscious of the preciousness of time now mine to share in loving service.

It is strange how some words seem to carry such great meaning. I have always liked the sound of the word "wholeness." Hearing the word, speaking it and writing it lift my spirit and urge me on to to greater things. Christian living seems to be a constant struggle for wholeness in the Spirit of Jesus. Wholeness of Christian vision as I view myself, my brothers and sisters, the whole of creation. Wholeness in Christian experience in the here-and-now. Wholeness in treasured relationships wherein I am able to love now as I will someday love in eternity. Wholeness in loving service in the daily struggle of self-giving (not always easy) and self-finding, my strengths and my weaknesses, hurt and hope, failure and forgiveness, pride and humility, death and resurrection.

Seeking wholeness in the Spirit is a continuing process of using my God-given creativity to seek out those in need of loving concern, serving them in the spirit of my Master, waiting for the Spirit to move in them and always rediscovering God's purpose in the shuffle of human affairs.

I look back to some forty-five years ago only to realize that resolutions made today were first made many years ago. I have without a doubt made progress, but I am ever thankful for each new day. It is the old story of struggling with the contradictions found within myself. The Spirit wants to move in one direction, toward wholeness of vision, but at times I am utterly distracted by the impulses of my human condition. Sometimes it will take hours to get back on the right track, to arrive at proper balance, to seek first the kingdom of God.

Tomorrow will give me another opportunity to experience Christian wholeness in my contacts with my brothers and sisters who so often feel unimportant or, by force of circumstances, are made to sit on the sidelines with little hope in the future. I am called to reach out to all men, the mighty, the forgotten, the saints and the sinners, the pleasant, the malcontent.

I look forward to another opportunity to express my gratitude to those who, bearing with my contradictions and weaknesses, have remained close at my side in loving concern. I will seek greater wholeness in these treasured relationships. Love for one another is a gift freely given. I cherish the moments of sharing with one who accepts me where I am and urges me on to greater things. I reveal my inner feelings, my frustrations, my hopes for the future, my determination to seek my Lord and my God before all else. I seek, I yearn, for wholeness of relationship.

In wholeness of service I find my greatest challenge. I often grow weary along the way. As a priest you hear for the greater part the defeats suffered by your people. It is not difficult to say Mass with devotion, to hear confessions with attentiveness, to instruct the little ones in Christian belief. It is far more difficult to become intimately involved in the lives of others. I am called to give of myself for the long haul in many and varied ways. However, it is when I go tht extra mile in loving service that I experience here and now the preciousness of the human person and the priceless gift of being a mediator between God and my brothers and sisters.

Christian wholeness in its fullness is found in the gathering of life, with all its richness and in all its struggle, in daily living out the mission and message of Jesus. August Bournonville, late leader of the Royal Danish Ballet, has said of ballet what could also be said of struggles for Christian wholeness: "Noble simplicity will always be beautiful. The astonishing, on the contrary, soon becomes boring."

A few years ago an old, discarded chalice was sent to me for proper disposal. At one time it had been a beautiful piece of handcrafted art, but now it was dented, tarnished and had seen much hard wear over one hundred or so years. My first thought was to have it melted down so the remaining silver and gold could be used to replate chalices in better condition. After some thought, I resolved to have the chalice repaired no matter what the cost. It had served well to hold the Precious Blood; it deserved a new tomorrow to again serve the Lord.

The chalice was replated, dents removed, stones replaced and small medallions of the four evangelists re-etched. This chalice is now used on Sundays at Our Lady of the Lake Church in Lake of the Ozarks, Missouri. Over 1,300 worshipers see the chalice raised before their eyes at each Mass.

The story of this particular chalice has real meaning for me every time I lift it high. It could easily have been cast aside, melted down, never to serve in the same fashion again. The same can be said of me. If I had given up when the bottom seemed to fall out, if those near to me had written me off as a lost cause, where would I be this day? By the grace of God, by the helping hands of many, I am daily being renewed in the Spirit. The bruises are continuously being healed. I constantly make every effort to put on the new man. All this takes persevering effort. It would be much easier to endure the dents, be content with myself, remain stagnant until my turn at the melting pot came along. I would at that time, unless totaly deluded, suffer regret, but there would be little I could do about it. I would have failed in my mission. My people would have suffered greatly from my lack of spiritual commitment.

The chalice was resurrected. The same can be accomplished for me if I address myself to the daily task of putting on the mind of Jesus. In my life, unpolished as it may seem at times, it is Jesus who surrounds me and whispers in my ear, time and time again, "Don't quit. Begin again." And as I do, Jesus augments and supplements my efforts until works of amazing beauty are accomplished in me.

To remain ever alive to the spirit of my calling as a Christian, as a priest, I seek out the moments of silence — quiet time wherein I look at Jesus and Jesus looks at me. In silence, I see more clearly my strengths and weaknesses. If I am truly seeking first the kingdom of God, then He will reveal to me His Spirit. I will not be deceived nor deceive. In silence I will see the changes to be made in my manner of living. The strength to make necessary changes — even radical changes — will be given me. I will grow in the love of God, the love of my neighbor in proportion to my willingness to remove from my eyes the scales that hamper me.

I humbly seek the help of someone walking the same path as I. Admitting my weaknesses openly to another pilgrim will make me mindful of the opportunities that come my way each day to think, speak and act as Jesus would think, speak and act. I need my friend to encourage me along the path to nobility of spirit, which in turn will demand a greater spirit of sacrifice on my part. Murray Banks, a Jewish psychiatrist, recalled a dairy farm with a sign that read, "Our cows are not contented, but always striving to do better."

I will live life one day at a time, knowing that the opportunities before me this day may never again cross my path. How often I've awakened in the morning to the news, "Did you hear? Father so-and-so died in his sleep!" In stark reality, father's time to live out the mission of Jesus ceased. The book was closed. I then realize how precious now is, the sanctity of this moment. I may show this by the simple greeting I give the housekeeper on our first meeting this day. It may be the words of encouragement I give to someone carrying a heavy burden. It may be the understanding I show the penitent, the concern I reveal for someone hurting in mind and heart, the depth of conviction I manifest when saying Mass, the need I feel within for lifting my mind and heart in prayer frequently during the day.

As a Servant I have witnessed over and over again priests who have, from all outward appearances, given up their desire to walk in the footsteps of their Master, only to see them renewed in their commitment to Jesus as the way, the truth and the life. One priest mentioned to me that he felt he had been reordained. The chalice has been given another opportunity to serve; the priest has been given new life in the spirit of his calling.

11

The Way, the Truth and the Life

A Hasidic Rabbi, Susya of Hanipol, on his deathbed explained to his students that he was not afraid that God would ask him why he was not Moses or Isaiah or Maimonides. He was afraid of only one question: "Susya, why weren't you Susya?"

For the last six weeks I have been visiting a young man who is in an alcohol and drug abuse center. Each Sunday I arrive at 1:00 p.m. Before I am able to visit my friend I am required to listen to a lecture on videotape. The presentation usually centers around how the family of an alcoholic or drug dependent can very easily be caught up in the sickness. The family can begin to think, speak and act as codependents even though the other members of the family are in no way addicted to either alcohol or drugs. I have seen these tapes many times over the past fifteen years. Last Sunday I was perturbed that on a very hot Sunday afternoon in Missouri I was being asked to view another tape I had already seen many times.

I knew there was no way out, so I put on my mask of acceptance. The lecture was by Father Ralph Martin, a dynamic speaker well versed on the subject of alcohol and drug abuse. I dutifully watched the tape, recalling many of father's jokes. The tape was excellent even on the tenth viewing, but it was Father Martin's closing testimony that made the entire forty-five minutes worthwhile. It was not an earth-shattering new thought, but my spirit was struck by his simple statement: "I believe there is a God. I believe He loves me."

If I truly believe these two statements then I am blessed abundantly with a living purpose that brings meaning and fulfillment to all I am and do.

I believe there is a God. I believe Jesus Christ to be His only begotten Son. I believe my Lord came into the world as the ultimate expression of God's love for every man and woman with *no* exceptions. The gospel — the Good News of my Lord's first coming —is the word of the living God. I seek with all my heart to follow in His footsteps even if I am the only one to make the journey. I pray for the depth of faith to move me daily to live out my faith. "I am the way, the truth and the life." I pray to stand before the nakedness of the Gospel and claim it as my own way, truth and life. I may stumble many times but my Lord will draw glory out of my falls. Not to be downcast after falling but to get up again and continue the journey is a mark of true holiness.

It follows, as day does night, that my belief in a loving God gives real power to my prayer life. To pray honestly is to pray dangerously. Communication with my Lord will not permit me to settle for mediocrity when I know I am called to a royal priesthood, a holy nation, a chosen race, a people set apart. In honest prayer there is a quality of boldness. I am urged to go far beyond previous limits of endurance and accomplishments. My union with my Lord provides power to achieve inner peace and determination in the very midst of a complex and often confusing world. I do not detour in my desire to follow my Lord. In the very center of having careful plans upset, dreams shattered, relationships broken, cherished programs scrapped, I am at peace in accepting what I cannot change. The compelling will of my God is revealed. I will cooperate with all He desires for me. My loving relationship with my Lord gives me the courage to walk fearlessly in His footsteps.

I believe in God's love for me. I believe all my brothers and sisters are created to His image. Who are my brothers and sisters? The image of Jesus was revealed in the face of the leper that Francis of Assisi held in his arms. At our county jail I met a young man who had raped a girl. He is my brother. I see the image of my Lord in him. The one who judges me before he has the facts is still my brother. The prodigal son who rebuffs me is still my son and I am ever ready to forgive. I will make every effort to separate the intent of their deed from the precious-ness of their creation. The hurt of their fall will be long enduring but I pray they experience the inner healing of forgiveness as I have so often been forgiven.

I cannot exclude anyone from my love and respect. Each person who enters my life, even for a brief moment, is a gift sent by my Lord. He or she may be the last person ever to enter my life. I am to take no one for granted.

Someone who merely claims to be a Christian in name only and who shows no real commitment to a change of life is an empty shell. He believes in Jesus in word but betrays disbelief in not accepting Jesus as the way, the truth, the life.

The greatest evil afflicting our world is not denial of Christian values but indifference on the part of those who have received the Good News but fail to act upon it. If my faith in Jesus is a reality in my life, if Jesus is the way, the truth and the life, then I must believe with all my being and make daily effort to put my belief into practice, even if I am called to travel the road alone.

The vitality of Christian belief can actually be threatened by an overemphasis on fulfillment of custom and ritual, lacking spirit and life. I can just be present for Mass or it can be a precious time of worship that will strengthen me in my firm resolve, as I leave the church, to mirror Jesus in my words and actions in my home, neighborhood, and place of employment. My belief in Jesus is not just another religion but a way of life. Attending Mass — even saying Mass — can be an obligation expected of me, and I will feel better when this sacred rite has been fulfilled. But attending or saying Mass in a spirit of worship cannot but help me more courageously live out the mission and message of Jesus no matter what obstacles I encounter. I can be quick to acknowledge the miraculous aspects of the life of Jesus and yet remain indifferent to His call to minister to others. I have been branded with the name of Jesus.

Poor leadership can cause spiritual indifference. If we who are called in a special way to minister to others find little fulfillment in the realm of the spiritual, how are we to urge our people on to greater things in the spirit? It is much easier to care for a parish complex than to spend time in quiet prayer, spiritual reading, preparation of a meaningful sermon. I cannot give what I do not have. Without a deep appreciation of prayer, without self-discipline, there is no way I can excite others to radical discipleship. Without any doubt there are many committed Christian leaders, but many more are needed to change the tide of indifference.

Living out my Christian commitment can be a daily challenge filled with vitality and varied experiences, bringing with it a great inner sense of fulfillment and peace, a peace the world cannot give. Such a spirit will inspire others. The people of our day long for what is enduring, for what will give real meaning to the most insignificant task when accepted by an all-loving Father, a Father in whose presence they live and receive their strength.

Throughout history, when spiritual indifference has eaten away at the very fabric of Christian idealism, men and women have come upon the scene to counter the sickness-unto-death of indifference. These men and women, often springing from the grass roots, have become the leaven of society. They are called to stir us up from complacency and urge us to open our hearts to the real values of life, seeking first the kingdom of God.

Our people hunger today for someone to simply speak to them of the love their Father has for them. They need to hear that they are accepted in their weakness and in their strength, with their unique capabilities. They must know they are truly accepted, held in His hands, affirmed in Him.

Thomas Merton said that all men and women are called to contemplation — a union with their Father in prayer. Have we leaders dared to challenge our people to a deeper appreciation of prayer? In quiet prayer new avenues of grace and enlightenment will be revealed to them. We never want to underestimate the miracles of grace worked in the lives of ordinary people set aflame by the personal experience of Jesus. A deeper appreciation of communion with God in prayer will bring about life-changing experiences in their lives and those they reach out to touch.

We ministers of the Word must go apart frequently to ask for the strength of purpose to grow in the love of Jesus and those entrusted to our care. Burnout is a reality. We *can* get tired of giving if we fail to minister to ourselves. Jesus frequently went apart from His disciples to speak openly to His Father. This does not necessarily mean we must leave our station. We can carry inner quietness into a distracting environment. As one spiritual writer so aptly put it, "If one cannot meditate in a boiler room, one cannot meditate." These moments apart will refresh our spirits to meet the next challenge.

I desire to live more fully in the presence of my Lord all the days of my life. In faith, I know Jesus is someone with whom I have a personal relationship. When I speak of Him, when I pronounce His name in prayer, when I bow my head at the mention of His name, my heart reveals an intimacy born of love.

To live in His presence I must first discern His plan for me. It is not difficult to walk in the footsteps of the Master as long as His footsteps are in cadence with mine. I must discern what is truly of God from what is of my own making. I kneel in His presence asking to be freed from all delusion, importance, preconceived answers and embedded prejudices so I can be open to hear the will of God. I am created to the image and likeness of my God. Too often I find myself thinking in reverse. I create God to my own image and likeness. It is easy to put the stamp of God on my present mood or manner of thinking and interpret it as God's will. This presumption might be the greatest travesty of religious belief for all of us. Not all those who say "Lord, Lord," will enter the kingdom — only those who do His will.

In times of quiet prayer I often find myself reflecting on certain symbolic gestures made during Mass. One symbolic gesture is made every time the Gospel — the word of Jesus — is proclaimed at Holy Mass. The priest or deacon and the faithful make a small cross on their foreheads, their lips, and their hearts before the words of the Gospel are read. We pray silently, "May the Gospel be in my mind, on my lips and in my heart."

When I make the cross on my forehead I beg for the gift to understand the words of Jesus as they apply to my life and the lives of those to whom I proclaim His message. Unless the words of Jesus are branded in my heart, any honest, enduring attempt at Christian commitment will be in vain. To profess to be a Christian and yet to have little interest in reading Holy Scripture is a grave contradiction. I have always admired the faithfulness of our Protestant brethren to the Bible. The Word of God is at the very heart of my calling as a priest, as one committed to Jesus, my Lord and my God. The Scriptures are at my side during the day. They rest at my bedside during the night. They are a treasured possession keeping me ever conscious of God's presence in my life. Whenever I become too involved in the hustle and bustle of everyday living, the reading of Holy Scripture brings me back to the reality of my calling to be a servant in imitation of my Master.

As I trace the sign of the cross on my lips I am grateful for the gift of proclaiming the Word. The day will come when I will no longer be able to hold in my hands the readings of Sacred Scripture. My lips will be silent. This is the appointed time for me to read the Word of God with deep conviction. This is the time for me to accept His words and to proclaim them with a strength of faith that will touch the hearts of my brothers and sisters. Of all that has been written from the beginning of time to this very day, the words of Holy Scripture alone consistently bring spirit and life into my ever searching mind and into my world of confused values. The Word of God is to permeate all that I do and say in the small and great of everyday living. Jesus must increase. I must decrease.

The cross I make reverently over my heart brings to mind the personal love my Lord has for me. I often reflect that Jesus would have suffered His passion and death on the cross if I had been the only person on earth. This means I would have had to drive the nails into His hands to crucify Him, so He could die for me. He would have readily forgiven me and received me into His kingdom. This is how valuable we are to the God who created us to His image. I am loved by God in my uniqueness. I belong to the family of God. I am destined to spend eternity with God. "I have loved you with an everlasting love, so I am constant in my affection for you" (Jeremiah).

Certain words in Scripture ring with richness every time I read them. One such word is "abundant." "I have come not to destroy life but to give you abundant life." Each day of my allotted time is precious. I am urged to live the present moment abundantly — to the full — in the Lord. Another word filled with profound meaning is "abide." It was used by Paul to refer to possessions of eternal value. "There abideth faith, hope and love, and the greatest of these is love." I gain new strength in the realization that faith, hope and love will abide with me now and in the kingdom.

Some twenty years ago my family bought a farm outside St. Louis. Dad wanted to set up a preserve for the wildlife that roamed the woods and open fields. A conservation officer visited the farm and gave us some practical suggestions on wildlife conservation. I will never forget his parting words. "Remember, we don't own the ground under our feet. We are but tenants preparing the ground for those to come after us." Material possessions are temporarily placed in our care. They will not abide with us forever. They too will pass.

As the years go by I become ever more conscious of how quickly those things I can feel, see and touch pass from view. What seemed so important in my younger days no longer abides with me. Clothes go out of style. Cars wear out. Physical strength weakens.

Recently I finished reading the life of General Douglas McArthur, a man who captured the hearts of many. The thunderous applause of those who admired him is now silent.

Cardinal Mundelein of Chicago was a powerful churchman in his time. As a young priest I was stationed in Chicago. No one knew what to do with the many oil paintings and prints of this renowned prelate. They were stored away in the attics of rectories, convents and institutions throughout the Chicago area. The Cardinal's time had passed. Thus passes the glory of the world. This lesson made a lasting impression on me.

Paul was inspired to write of those treasured virtues that "moth or rust" cannot destroy. They are faith, hope and love. These are the keys to the kingdom.

I must seek with firm and persevering purpose to know Jesus, His mission, His message. I have read over and over again the Bible and especially the New Testament, but reading, hearing does not for me necessarily indicate a genuine penetration and acceptance of His message as the *only* way, truth and life that will bring inner fulfillment to myself and those I serve.

If I believe my God is merciful, forgiving, and loving, then I will have no doubt that my sins and the sins of my brothers and sisters are forgiven like straw thrown into the fire. I will not allow myself to be crippled by guilt trips. In faith, I will begin anew each day confident of God's forgiveness for all who seek it with a humble heart. Peter walked with Jesus, talked with Jesus, witnessed scores of miracles and yet denied Jesus. What a great consolation to know he sought forgiveness and received it instantly.

If I believe Jesus is the Son of God, *if I believe* His message is proclaimed in the Gospels, then every word Jesus spoke will be burned into my heart.

If I believe in His real presence it will be evident to all by the reverence of my genuflection, by my fervor when I pronounce the words of consecration, and by the devotion with which I place the sacred host upon the tongue or in the hands of all those receiving His body and blood. If I open up the floodgates in my heart and allow the power of Jesus' real presence to work in me, then Jesus will be revealed in all I do and say.

It is no great personal, spiritual achievement to say Mass daily unless I make every effort to live out the redeeming power of Mass each day. Lifting my mind and heart to God in silent prayer throughout the day, times set aside for spiritual reading and meditation — these may seem restrictive of my time, but without this liberating daily experience, am I truly free to live in the Spirit of my Redeemer?

I seek to be free to live each precious day of my life in His presence. The efforts made will not only redound to my good but to the good of those I am called to serve. The closing words of His high priestly prayer will constantly be on my lips: "Father, for them do I sanctify myself." On the night before my Master's death there were no words of self-pity. He commended himself into His Father's hands and freely offered himself for His friends, my people.